90 MINUTES

Published 2006 by Merrell Publishers Limited

Head office
81 Southwark Street
London SE1 0HX

New York office
49 West 24th Street, 8th Floor
New York, NY 10010

www.merrellpublishers.com

Publisher Hugh Merrell
Editorial Director Julian Honer
US Director Joan Brookbank
Sales and Marketing Manager Kim Cope
Sales and Marketing Assistant Abigail Coombs
Managing Editor Anthea Snow
Project Editor Claire Chandler
Junior Editor Helen Miles
Art Director Nicola Bailey
Designer Paul Shinn
Production Manager Michelle Draycott
Production Controller Sadie Butler

British Library Cataloguing-in-Publication Data:
90 minutes : the greatest moments from the World Cup
1.World Cup (Soccer) – History – Pictorial works
I.Davies, Robert II.Williams, Richard III.Ninety minutes
796.3'34668'0222

ISBN 1 85894 305 1

Commissioned by Mark Fletcher
Designed by Atelier Works
Edited by Helen Miles

Printed and bound in China

The Greatest Moments from the World Cup
Robert Davies

Build up **Gianluca Vialli**
Commentary **Richard Williams**

PROGRAMME

The Argentinian crowd

Argentina v Holland
3–1 AET (Final)
25 June 1978
Attendance 77,260
Monumental
Buenos Aires, Argentina

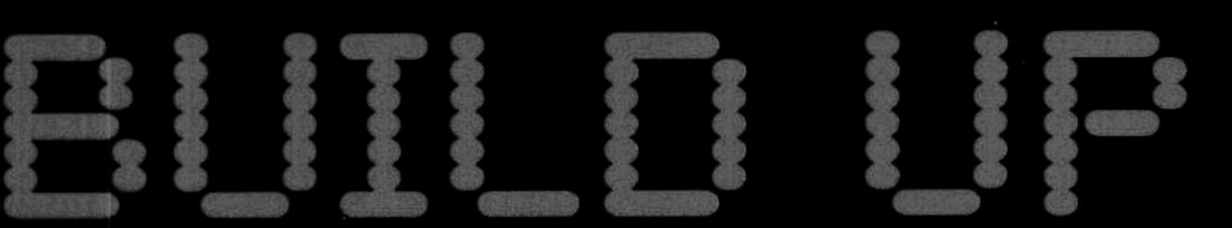

Gianluca Vialli

The Romanian team

Romania v Sweden
2–2 AET (Quarter-final)
Sweden 5–4 on penalties
10 July 1994
Attendance 81,715
Rose Bowl
Pasadena, USA

The first time I saw Robert Davies's work I was struck by two opposing feelings. One was familiarity: his images are familiar, both in terms of subject-matter and setting. In fact, because they are taken from the television, they are recognized by football fans everywhere. Everybody who watches the World Cup, apart from the few tens of thousands of spectators in the ground itself, views exactly the same pictures. So, in looking at the images, I felt I was visiting a place where I had been before. Yet, at the same time, there was a sense of discovery, as if I were contemplating these pictures for the first time.

While looking at Robert's image of Zinédine Zidane, for example, I was seeing Zidane as I had never seen him before, thanks to the editing and cropping of the frame. Not only that, but he appeared more real to me. The Zidane in Robert's work, strange as it may sound, is more Zidane than the Zidane found in a conventional photograph. Perhaps it represents him in a better way than Zidane would be able to convey in person.

Is this a contradiction? Yes, it is. How can Zidane seem new and familiar at the same time? How can Robert's version be more accurate than the real thing? I am no art critic, but I think the answer lies in what art is, or more specifically, this kind of art. To me it is the manipulation of an image that creates something that is more real than reality. And that is why it is powerful – at least to me. They say a picture is worth a thousand words. Without question a good photograph can convey an emotion, but a great photograph can go further, soliciting and fostering an emotion in the viewer. But it takes an artist of Robert's talent, vision and patience to manipulate the familiar into something that elicits a response, and at the same time represents the complexity of a short passage of time in a still image.

As someone who loves football, this is what I appreciate most: the complexity in Robert's art. Because football is not just a game, it's an experience that exists at the point where athleticism, emotion, technique, culture, art and humanity meet. And to me all this is apparent in his work.

COMMENTARY

Richard Williams

A man in a red shirt kneels on the grass, his shadow stretching in front of him, his expression hidden. His hands are on his knees. He could be praying or mourning. Two white lines, one straight and the other an arc, form a complex geometry with the straight edge of his arms and the curve of his body. The grass appears scorched by the late-afternoon sun; divots scar the surface, each casting its own little shadow. This is the greatest moment of the man's life.

England have just won the World Cup for the first and, so far, the only time, and Jack Charlton has played his part as one of the eleven men who will go on to assume a special position in the nation's memory. The tall, giraffe-necked, raw-boned Jack, the centre-half in Alf Ramsey's team and brother of the more famous Bobby, is a familiar figure; we are used to seeing film of him rising from a crowded penalty area to head a cross away from danger, brushing an opponent aside with the minimum of *politesse*, cajoling his teammates with what we might guess to be a harsh north-eastern tongue. What Robert Davies does with this simple image, however, takes us to another level of understanding.

In this instant, England's moment of triumph, Jack Charlton's head is filled with thoughts and feelings so unique to his experience that they are impossible to articulate. By taking this image from a videotape of the World Cup final of 1966, by isolating it and treating it in a way that enhances its inherent qualities, Robert Davies reveals something more of what Charlton thought and felt as that day at Wembley reached its climax. There is loneliness in failure, but there is a kind of loneliness in success too: a sudden hollowness at the moment of triumph, with the expected explosion of joy delayed for a second by the realization that the journey is over. Here is the elder Charlton, caught in that unrepeatable, unfathomable instant.

To anyone who watches the game in the spirit of the love and commitment of a true fan, the idea of football itself – as opposed to the experience of going to a match or of dancing in the streets in celebration of a win – exists largely as a sequence of isolated moments in which individual players reached an expressive peak. The clearest of these remembered incidents are derived from our direct experiences as spectators; many of them, inevitably, will date from childhood and adolescence, when events can imprint themselves on our memories with unusually lasting clarity. But since the things we have glimpsed are not always viewed from a helpful vantage point, they can become blurred, distorted by our subsequent interpretation. What we have seen becomes what we think we saw. The mind can manipulate an image, in a natural version of the digital processes used to adapt film, as if it were an animation. In the memory of a football fan, a goal seen from one angle can be turned around in the mind's eye, revealing another facet. We enhance our memories, as if turning up the brightness and contrast on a television screen, or replaying the incident via the footage from another camera.

Robert Davies's pictures, taken from film of sixteen of the seventeen World Cups held since the tournament was inaugurated in 1930, operate in this way: as recovered and enhanced memory. It is seldom first-hand memory, of course, and sometimes of events we cannot remember for ourselves in any authentic sense. Yet those of us who were unable to be among the crowd of more than 200,000 that overflowed the brand-new

Jack Charlton

England v West Germany
4–2 AET (Final)
30 July 1966
Attendance 93,802
Wembley
London, England

The Adidas ball

Argentina v Holland
0–4 (Group stage)
26 June 1974
Attendance 56,548
Gelsenkirchenstadion
Gelsenkirchen, West Germany

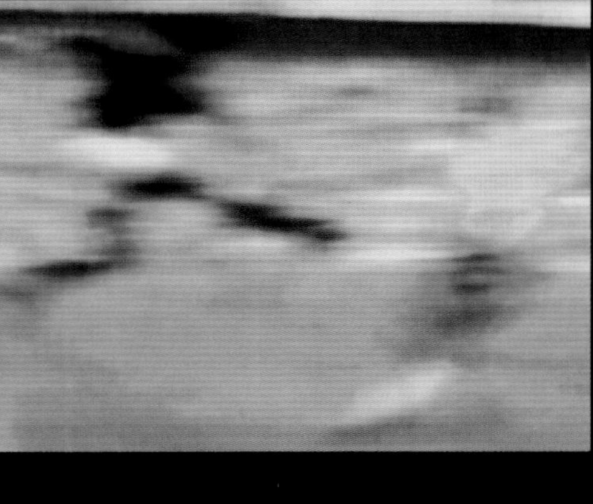

The final

Brazil v Italy
4–1 (Final)
21 June 1970
Attendance 107,412
Estadio Azteca
Mexico City, Mexico

Maracanã stadium in Rio de Janeiro for the final match of the first post-war tournament on 16 July 1950, or to witness the game on television, nevertheless can recognize a moment of history as we look at Davies's image. We see it in his interpretation of the low-angle shot of the ball that left the foot of Alcide Ghiggia, Uruguay's right-winger, and came to rest in the Brazilian goal, giving his country (a nation of no more than three million people) their second title, and striking the home supporters (who represented more than 100 million) dumb with horror.

By the use of various processes, including enlarging a detail and heightening the colour, sometimes rephotographing the frames time and again in order to accentuate some salient quality that has caught his eye, and taking advantage of the strange tonalities imparted to a black-and-white image by the 625 lines of a cathode-ray colour television screen, Davies aestheticizes and anatomizes his images. Throughout this collection, abstraction vies with a documentary element. Some of the frames are virtually purged of their meaning, while in others unexpected overtones come to the forefront. Within the frozen close-up of the referee Kim Milton Nielsen, filmed during a famous match in Saint-Etienne in 1998, we seem to glimpse a hint of uncertainty in his eyes, something that would not have been visible to the spectator at the time, either watching in the stadium or in front of a television. When he pulled out a card that night, in response to David Beckham's flick of a boot at Diego Simeone in the Stade Geoffroy-Guichard, did Nielsen really mean it to be the red one?

Robert Davies is not primarily a photographer, although much of his work is photography-based and it was with a medium-format camera that he captured, or perhaps we should say recaptured, the images that form this book. Born between the tournaments of 1962 and 1966, he studied at the Royal College of Art in London, graduating in 1993. Among his earliest works were huge close-ups of the human body, presented as landscapes. While employed as a cycle courier, he photographed formations of clouds, land and oceans from the windows of airliners, again creating pieces marked by their sense of adjusted scale. In 1999 he produced a series of pieces entitled *Water*, for which he used a digital camera to record the surfaces of ponds, lakes and rivers, then played the film back through a television set, rephotographed selected images with a still camera and manipulated the results to take them far beyond their origins. More recently, he has worked with a Formula One racing team, taking photographs of the tiniest details of their cars, and turning the lens of a rain light, a circuit board, the grain of tyre rubber and the fine pleating of an oil radiator into absorbing frames that are very distant from the banality of the images that emerge by the thousand from the Grand Prix world.

In 1997 Davies began working on a long-term project that became known as *Epiphany*, in which he created unexpected images by manipulating film of the World Cup tournaments. The works from this project now form this book. "Sport is my passion," he told me, "and the World Cup is a culturally significant event that reaches everyone, even people who aren't interested in football." What the project is about, he says, is "taking a bit of visual information and making it into something more testing and perhaps more sophisticated. And as I worked over a period of many months,

9
tional Stadium

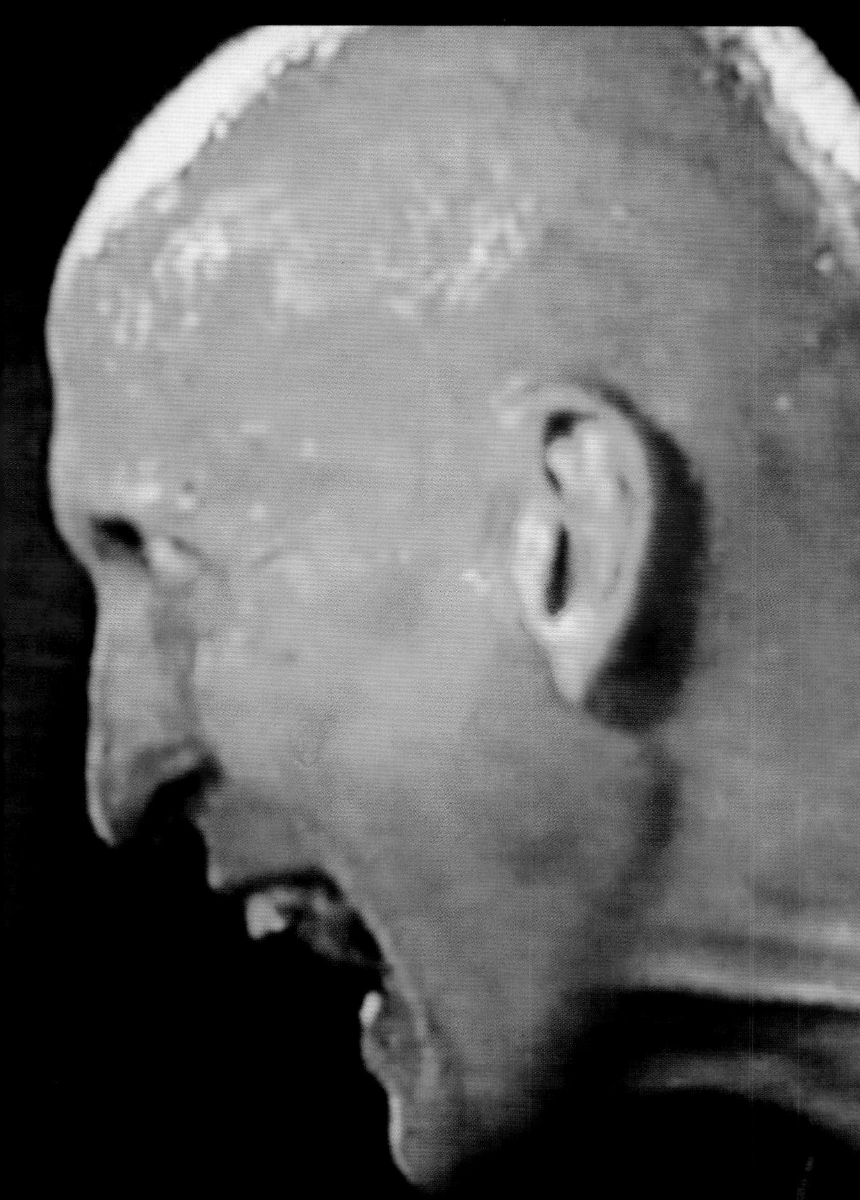

rephotographing the images time and again, I began to realize that the more abstracted they became, the more satisfying they were as pieces of art."

Some of these images can only be described as 'painterly'. The stocky outline of Diego Maradona, caught in mid-slalom through the England defence in 1986, on his way to scoring one of the most famous goals of all time, is reduced to a sketch of movement and balance that resembles one of Matisse's jazz dancers, who are also recalled in Johan Neeskens's joyful leap as he celebrates the first goal in Holland's win over Brazil in their quarter-final of 1974. Pelé's run at the Bulgarian defence in 1966, with the ball at his feet, uses the transformation of a black-and-white image on a colour television screen to produce a picture that is reminiscent of the abstraction of Monet's water lilies. Pelé is a recurrent presence in the series, and as Gordon Banks leaps to turn away his header in the sunshine of Guadalajara in 1970, the great contemporary German artist Gerhard Richter comes to mind, and not for the only time in looking through this collection. Elsewhere, as in the portrait of Gerd Müller against a background of spectators, the streaks and daubs of colour evoke the mature Post-Impressionism of Cézanne and the developments of Nicolas de Staël (who produced a celebrated sequence of canvases after watching France lose to Sweden under floodlights in the Parc des Princes, Paris, in 1952).

In other frames, searching for a different response, Davies pushes even further beyond the content of the image and all narrative is stripped away as he produces something that approaches pure abstraction. A sea of red shirts and white flags

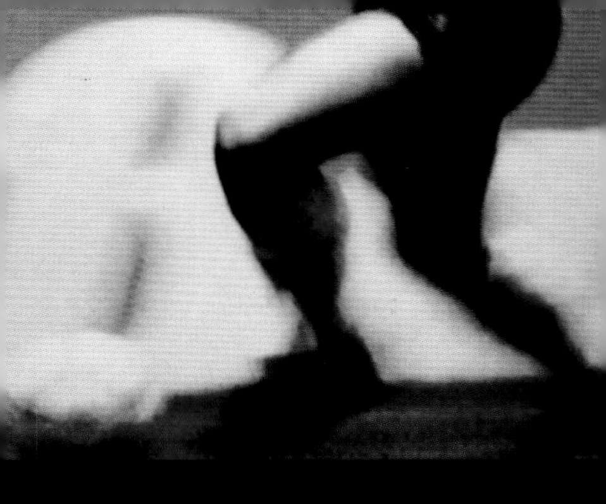

Diego Maradona

Argentina v England
2–1 (Quarter-final)
22 June 1986
Attendance 114,580
Estadio Azteca
Mexico City, Mexico

David Beckham

England v Nigeria
0–0 (Group stage)
12 June 2002
Attendance 44,864
Nagai Stadium
Osaka, Japan

The Germans, however, had other ideas. Three goals, feverish defending and a Welsh linesman whose offside decision denied Puskás a late equalizer brought them their first World Cup.

Brazil got their hands on the trophy for the first time in Sweden in 1958, thanks to the first of their great squads, including the forwards Vavá, Garrincha and the seventeen-year-old Pelé. Brought into the side after a goalless group match against England, Pelé and Garrincha revitalized the team. Pelé scored his first goal in the 1–0 quarter-final victory over Wales, notched a hat-trick in the 5–2 victory over France in the semi-final and scored another pair as the host nation went down 5–2 in the final. For the first of those, ten minutes into the second half, he flicked it over the head of a defender with his thigh, and volleyed the dropping ball past the Swedish goalkeeper.

Pelé also scored for Brazil in their opening match four years later in Chile, as they beat Mexico 2–0. But in the second game, a goalless draw against Czechoslovakia, his groin gave way in the act of shooting and his tournament was over. Garrincha took over as Brazil made their way through the later stages, scoring twice against Chile in the semi-final but leaving it to Amarildo, Zito and Vavá as their side beat the Czechoslovaks 3–1 in the final.

When England's year came, in 1966, Pelé had been kicked out of the tournament by the Bulgarian and Portuguese defenders, Italy had been humbled by North Korea, a new generation of gifted Hungarians had been strong-armed by the Soviet Union, and Argentina had self-destructed against the hosts. Even in defeat, however, the seeds of a new Brazil had been sown, and the results were on view in Mexico in 1970, when Pelé was joined by Tostão, Jairzinho, Carlos Alberto and Rivelino in a team that reached new levels of skill and beauty. A hard-fought 1–0 win over Alf Ramsey's defending champions eventually led to a wonderfully authoritative 4–1 victory in the final over an Italian team that was good enough to have beaten West Germany 4–3 in a thunderous semi-final.

West Germany, on home ground, met Holland in 1974 in a final expected to confirm the brilliance of Cruijff and the 'Total Football' generation. Like Hungary in 1954, however, the Dutch failed to live up to their billing. When Berti Vogts fouled Cruijff after two minutes, Neeskens converted the penalty to give his team the earliest lead ever taken in a World Cup final, but strangely their early success seemed to demotivate the Dutch. Paul Breitner, football's most celebrated Maoist, equalized from the penalty spot, and the inevitable Müller grabbed the winner just before half time. Nor could the Dutch stop the hosts in 1978, when Argentina seemed possessed by an unearthly power as they swept to a 3–1 victory over their Cruijff-less opponents amid a blizzard of confetti in the Monumental in Buenos Aires.

Italy achieved a third victory in 1982, using fair means (Rossi's goals) and foul (Claudio Gentile's marking) to overcome the formidable Argentina and Brazil in their second-round group matches before beating West Germany 3–1 in the final. Maradona dominated the 1986 tournament in Mexico as conclusively as Pelé had done on the same ground sixteen years earlier, slaloming through the English and Belgian defences to score unforgettable goals before producing the pass

ohan Cruijff

Holland v West Germany
–2 (Final)
 July 1974
ttendance 77,833
Olympiastadion
Munich, West Germany

he Maracaná

razil v Uruguay
–2 (Final)
6 July 1950
ttendance 199,854
Maracaná
io de Janeiro, Brazil

from which Jorge Burruchaga scored the winning goal in Argentina's 3–2 victory over West Germany in the Estadio Azteca. Four years later the same two countries played out a far less distinguished match in Rome, decided by Andy Brehme's penalty as Maradona's Argentina became the first team to fail to score in a World Cup final.

In 1994 there was little better to be seen from Brazil and Italy in the final in Pasadena, settled in favour of the South Americans by a penalty shoot-out in which Roberto Baggio, the tournament's outstanding player, missed the decisive kick. The mysterious seizure suffered by Ronaldo on the morning of the 1998 final in Paris did not, in the end, prevent Brazil's star forward from taking part, but the whole team seemed diminished as France won 3–0 with two goals from Zidane and one from Emmanuel Petit. Ronaldo was back on form in Japan in 2002, however, scoring both goals in the final against Germany as a solid defence provided a platform for the creative skills of Ronaldinho and Rivaldo to bring Brazil their fifth title.

Those are the details. The poetry is in the pictures,

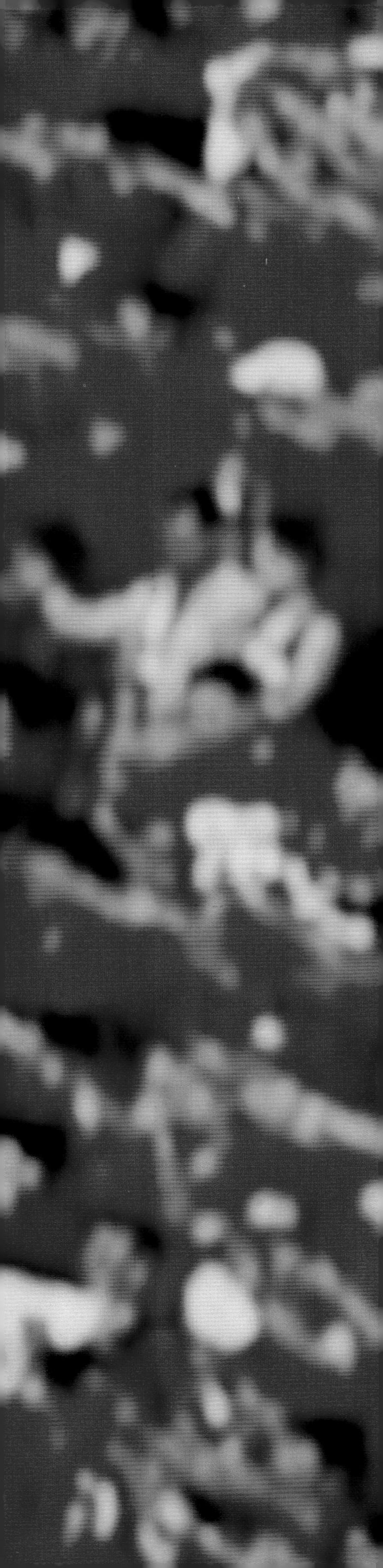

KICK

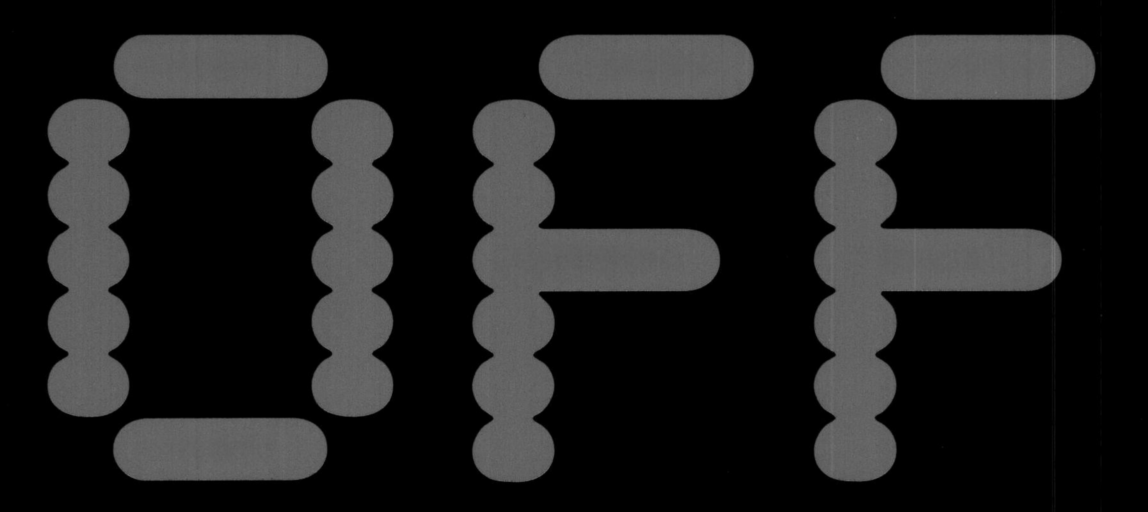
OFF

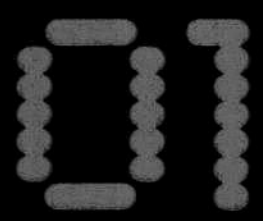

Kick off

The heavy, brown leather ball is splashed with whitewash prior to kick off for the final.

England v West Germany
4–2 AET (Final)
30 July 1966
Attendance 93,802
Wembley
London, England

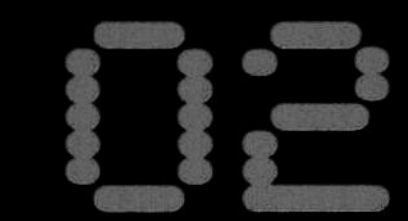

Johan Neeskens

From the kick off, Holland retain possession for more than a minute, Cruijff draws a foul from Vogts and Neeskens scores the penalty; West Germany haven't touched the ball: total football.

Holland v West Germany
1–2 (Final)
7 July 1974
Attendance 77,833
Olympiastadion
Munich, West Germany

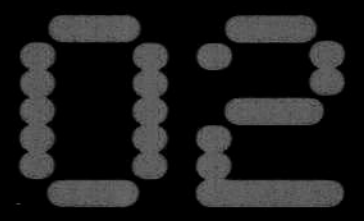

Vavá

Vavá volleys the first of Brazil's five goals that see them through to the final.

Brazil v France
5–2 (Semi-final)
24 June 1958
Attendance 27,100
Råsunda Stadion
Stockholm, Sweden

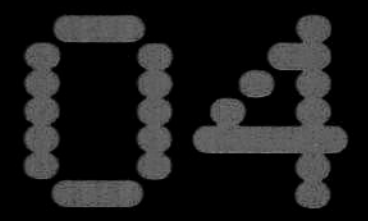

Fernando Hierro
Hierro lines up to shoot early in the first half as the sun goes down.

Spain v South Korea
2–2 (Group stage)
17 June 1994
Attendance 56,247
Cotton Bowl
Dallas, USA

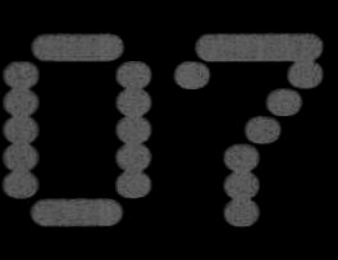

Battle of Santiago
Chile and Italy play one of the most ill-tempered games in the history of World Cup tournaments. The English referee Kenneth Aston sends off two Italians.

Chile v Italy
2–0 (Group stage)
2 June 1962
Attendance 66,057
Estadio Nacional
Santiago, Chile

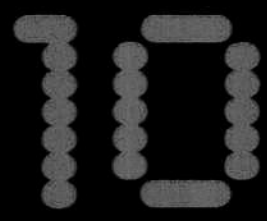

Gordon Banks

Pelé heads an almost certain goal into the bottom corner. Banks throws himself with unimaginable agility and tips the ball over the bar. It might be the greatest save ever seen.

England v Brazil
0–1 (Group stage)
7 June 1970
Attendance 70,950
Estadio Jalisco
Guadalajara, Mexico

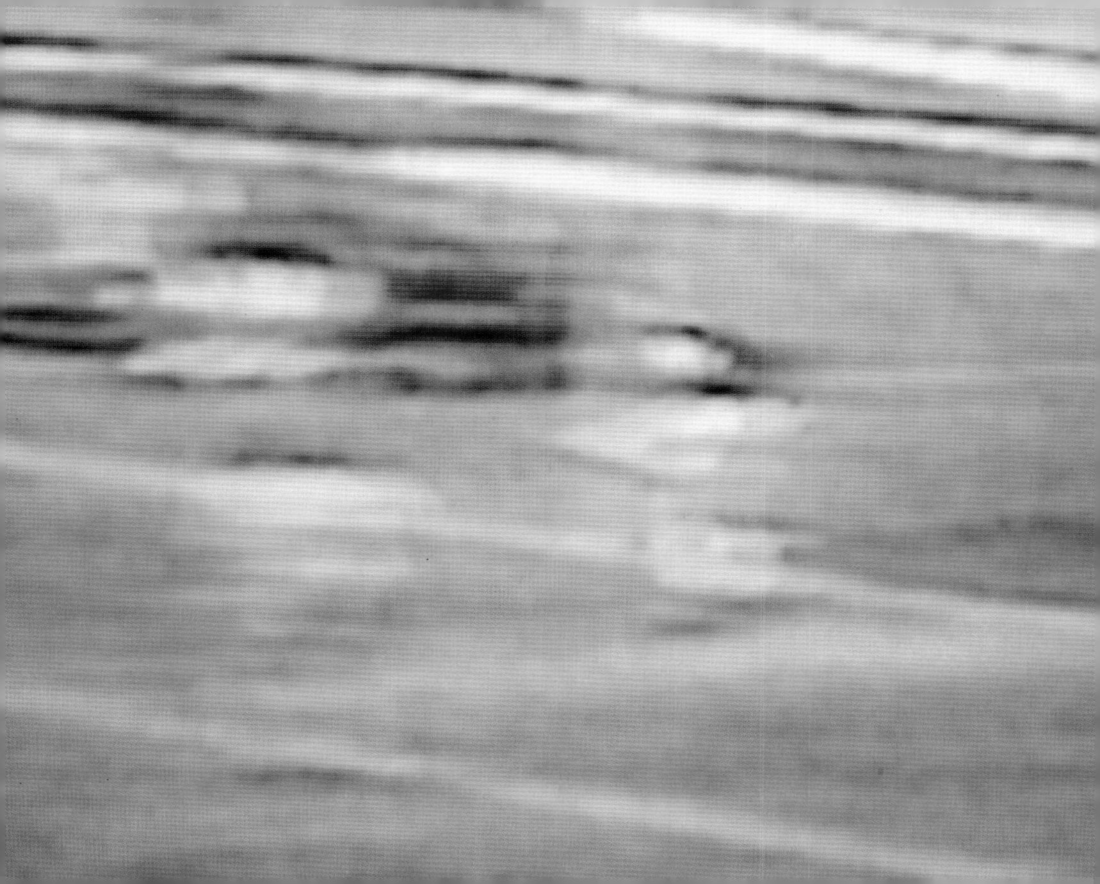

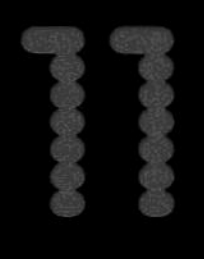

Rivelino
With the outside of his brutal left foot, Rivelino puts Brazil ahead.

Brazil v Peru
4–2 (Quarter-final)
14 June 1970
Attendance 54,000
Estadio Jalisco
Guadalajara, Mexico

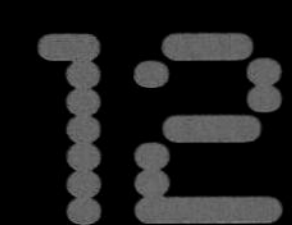

Socratés

Socratés works a neat 'one-two' with Zico and scores at Zoff's near post during a game in which Italy take the lead three times.

Brazil v Italy
2–3 (2nd round)
5 July 1982
Attendance 44,000
Estadio de Sarriá
Barcelona, Spain

14

Pelé

Pelé dribbles at the massed Bulgarian defence before driving into the area and scoring.

Brazil v Bulgaria
2–0 (Group stage)
12 July 1966
Attendance 47,308
Goodison Park
Liverpool, England

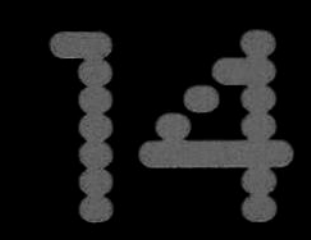

Marcel Desailly
Desailly brooks no argument in his desire to win a tackle. His commitment is not matched by his compatriots as the holders go out at the group stage.

France v Denmark
0–2 (Group stage)
11 June 2002
Attendance 48,100
Incheon Munhak Stadium
Incheon, South Korea

15

Just Fontaine

Fontaine scores the first of four goals against West Germany and goes on to become the highest scorer in a single World Cup tournament, with thirteen in total.

France v West Germany
6–3 (3rd place play-off)
28 June 1958
Attendance 32,483
Nya Ullevi Stadion
Gothenburg, Sweden

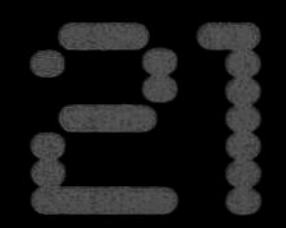

Frank Rijkaard and Rudi Völler
A frustrated Rijkaard spits at Völler before and after they are both sent off in this bitter game between neighbours.

Holland v West Germany
1–2 (2nd round)
24 June 1990
Attendance 74,559
San Siro
Milan, Italy

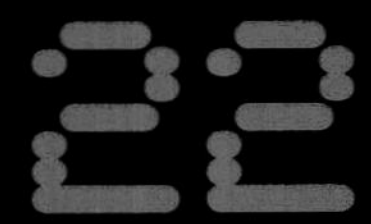

Fryderyk Scherfke

Scherfke is rugby-tackled by a Brazilian defender who doesn't seem to know the rules. He scores from the resulting penalty in a thrilling game decided by the odd goal.

Poland v Brazil
5–6 (Group stage)
7 June 1938
Attendance 13,452
Stade de la Meinau
Strasbourg, France

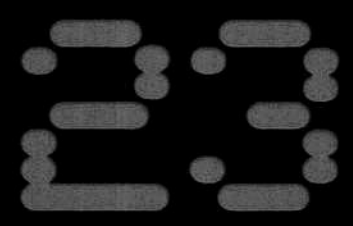

Johan Cruijff
Cruijff dummies to cross and with perfect balance executes what becomes known as the 'Cruijff turn'.

Holland v Sweden
0–0 (Group stage)
19 June 1974
Attendance 52,500
Westfalenstadion
Dortmund, West Germany

2D ROSSI
GOL

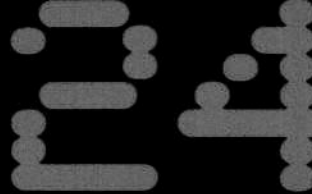

Paolo Rossi

Rossi scores the sec
of his fantastic hat-
beat the best Brazil
never to win the Wo
And this after he wa
from playing due to
scandal. The scoreb
flashes up Rossi's n
and number.

Italy v Brazil
3–2 (2nd round)
5 July 1982
Attendance 44,000
Estadio de Sarriá
Barcelona, Spain

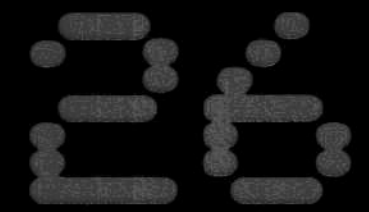

Eusébio

Eusébio heads the first of his brilliant double against Brazil that sees the holders knocked out.

Portugal v Brazil
3–1 (Group stage)
19 July 1966
Attendance 58,479
Goodison Park
Liverpool, England

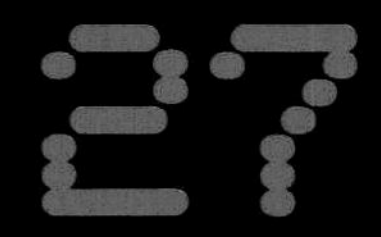

Julius Aghahowa

Aghahowa celebrates scoring in his unique fashion.

Nigeria v Sweden
1–2 (Group stage)
7 June 2002
Attendance 36,194
Kobe Wing Stadium
Kobe, Japan

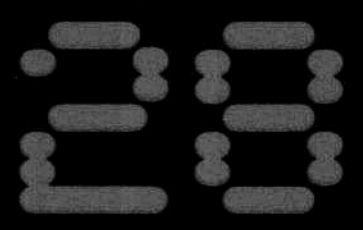

Eugenio Parlier
Parlier is unable to stop Wagner's shot as Austria come from 3–0 down to win this amazing match.

Switzerland v Austria
5–7 (Quarter-final)
26 June 1954
Attendance 32,000
Stade Olympique de la Pontaise
Lausanne, Switzerland

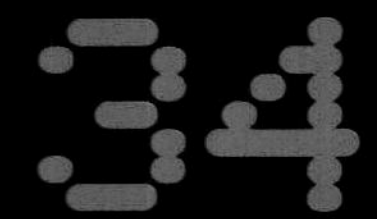

Andrés Escobar

After scoring an own goal that results in Colombia's failure to qualify from their group, Escobar looks haunted. He was assassinated a few days later when the team returned home.

Colombia v USA
1–2 (Group stage)
22 June 1994
Attendance 93,134
Rose Bowl
Pasadena, USA

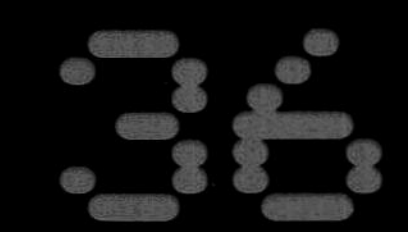

Zinédine Zidane

Zidane is the ultimate exponent of a game that is first mental, then physical.

France v Denmark
0–2 (Group stage)
11 June 2002
Attendance 48,100
Incheon Munhak Stadium
Incheon, South Korea

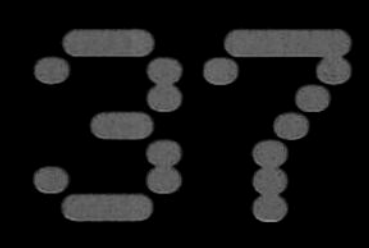

Roberto Boninsegna
Boninsegna equalizes for Italy against the formidable Brazilians.

Italy v Brazil
1–4 (Final)
21 June 1970
Attendance 107,412
Estadio Azteca
Mexico City, Mexico

11

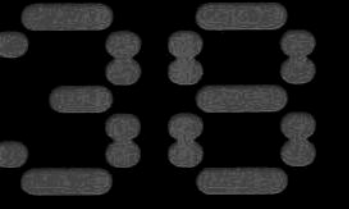

Ignacio Calderón and Bobby Charlton

Charlton drives from the halfway line and unleashes a trademark shot that bulges the Mexican net. Calderón dives in vain. It's one of the finest goals ever seen at Wembley and settles England's nerves in the group stages.

England v Mexico
2–0 (Group stage)
16 July 1966
Attendance 92,570
Wembley
London, England

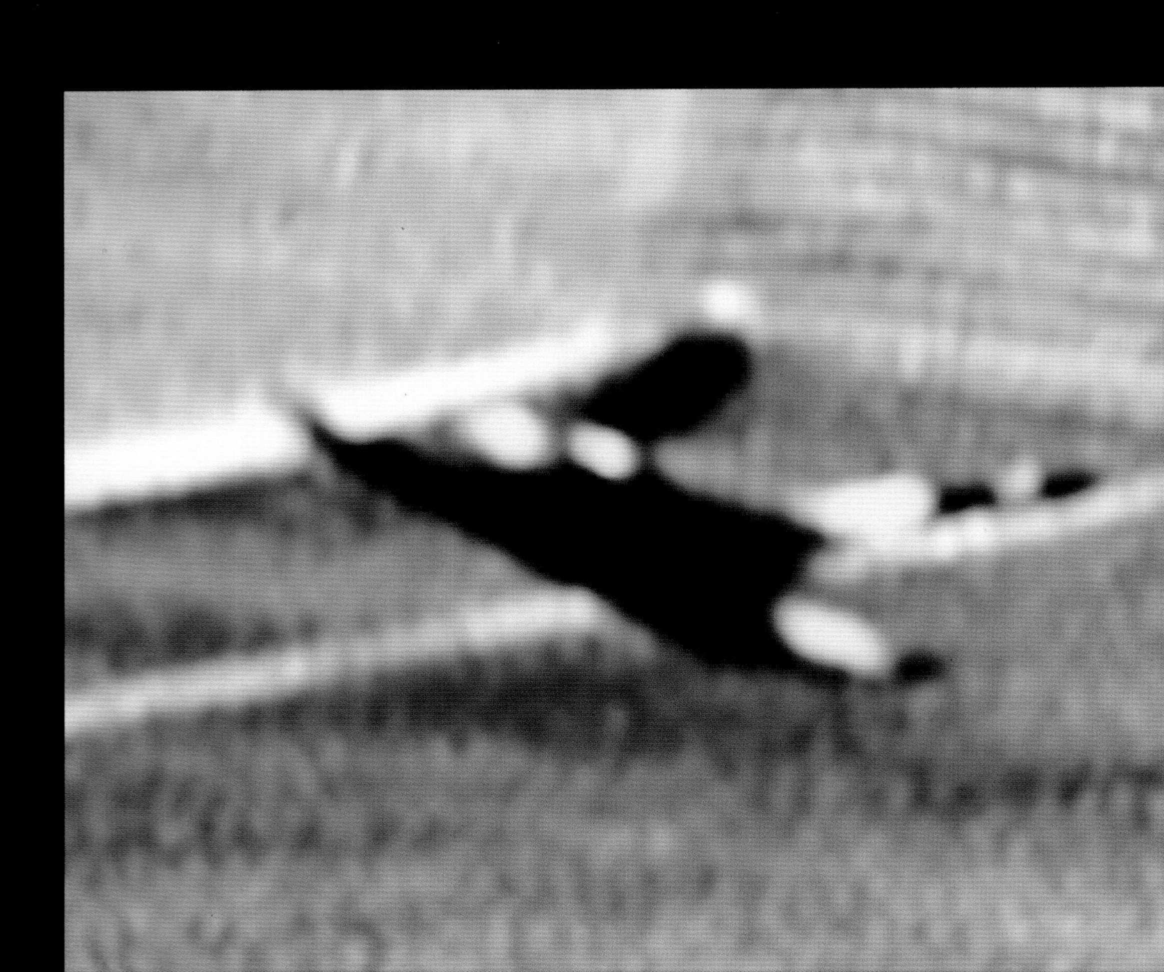

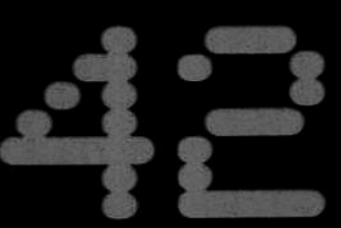

Pak Doo Ik

Pak scores the winner for North Korea in their hugely shocking win over Italy.

North Korea v Italy
1–0 (Group stage)
19 June 1966
Attendance 17,829
Ayresome Park
Middlesborough, England

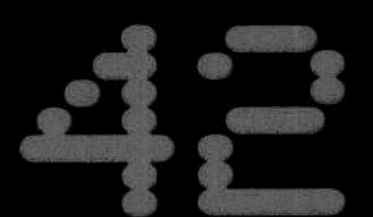

Ivo Viktor

Pelé shoots from inside his own half. The Czech goalie, Viktor, turns in horror but is pleased to see the ball pass just outside the post.

Brazil v Czechoslovakia
4–1 (Group stage)
3 June 1970
Attendance 52,897
Estadio Jalisco
Guadalajara, Mexico

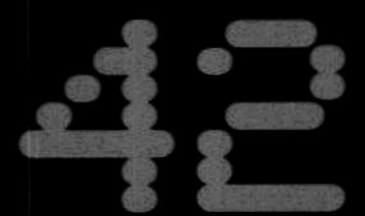

Jorge Toro

Toro bends a perfect free kick over the Brazilian wall. The home team think they can make the final.

Chile v Brazil
2–4 (Semi-final)
13 June 1962
Attendance 76,594
Estadio Nacional
Santiago, Chile

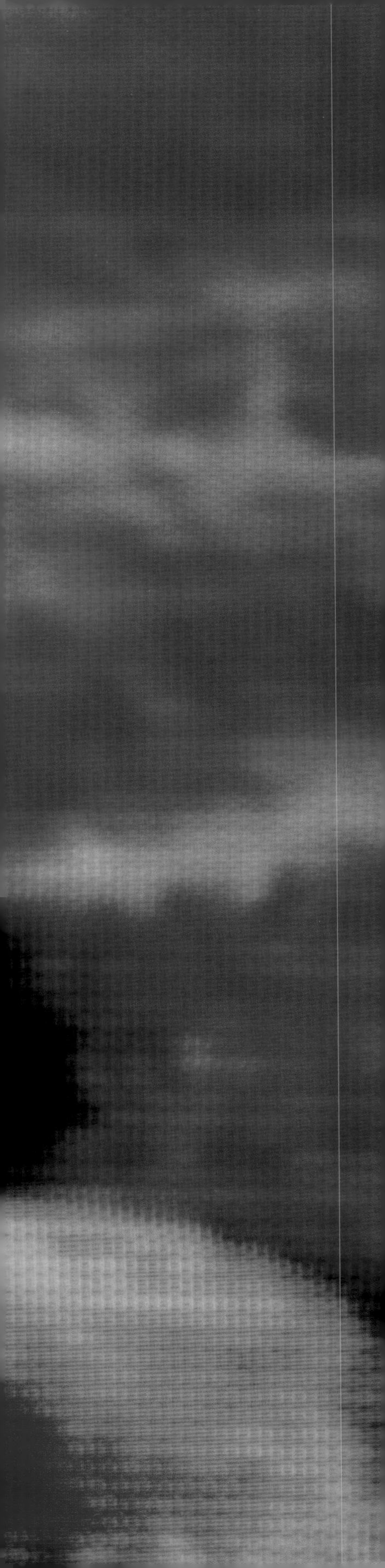

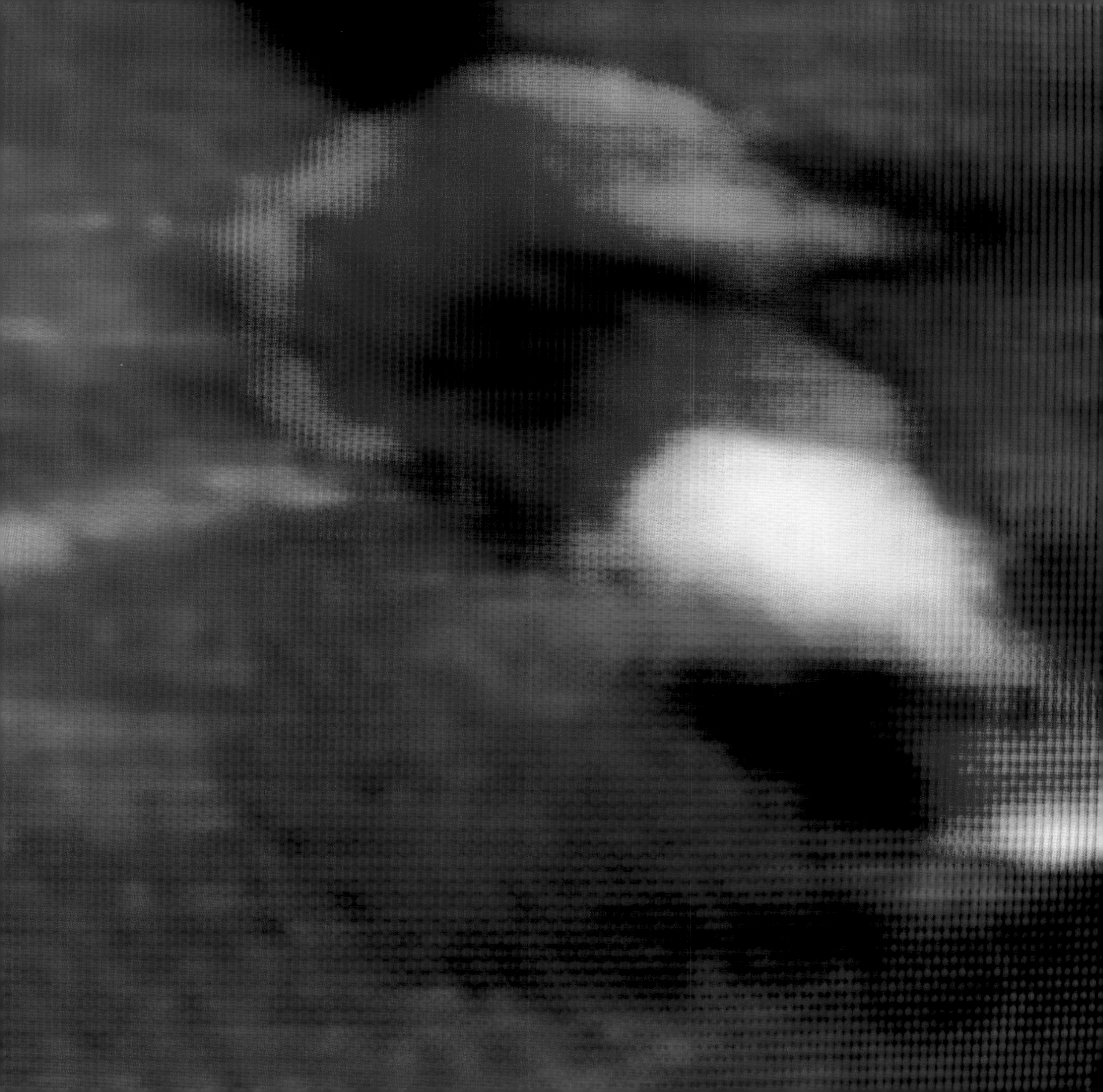

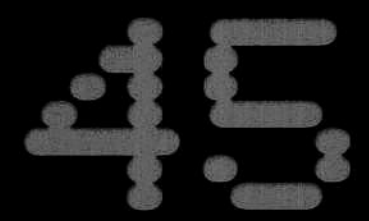

David Beckham
Beckham is overjoyed after scoring the penalty that sees England take revenge for their 1998 defeat.

England v Argentina
1–0 (Group stage)
7 June 2002
Attendance 35,927
Sapporo Dome
Sapporo, Japan

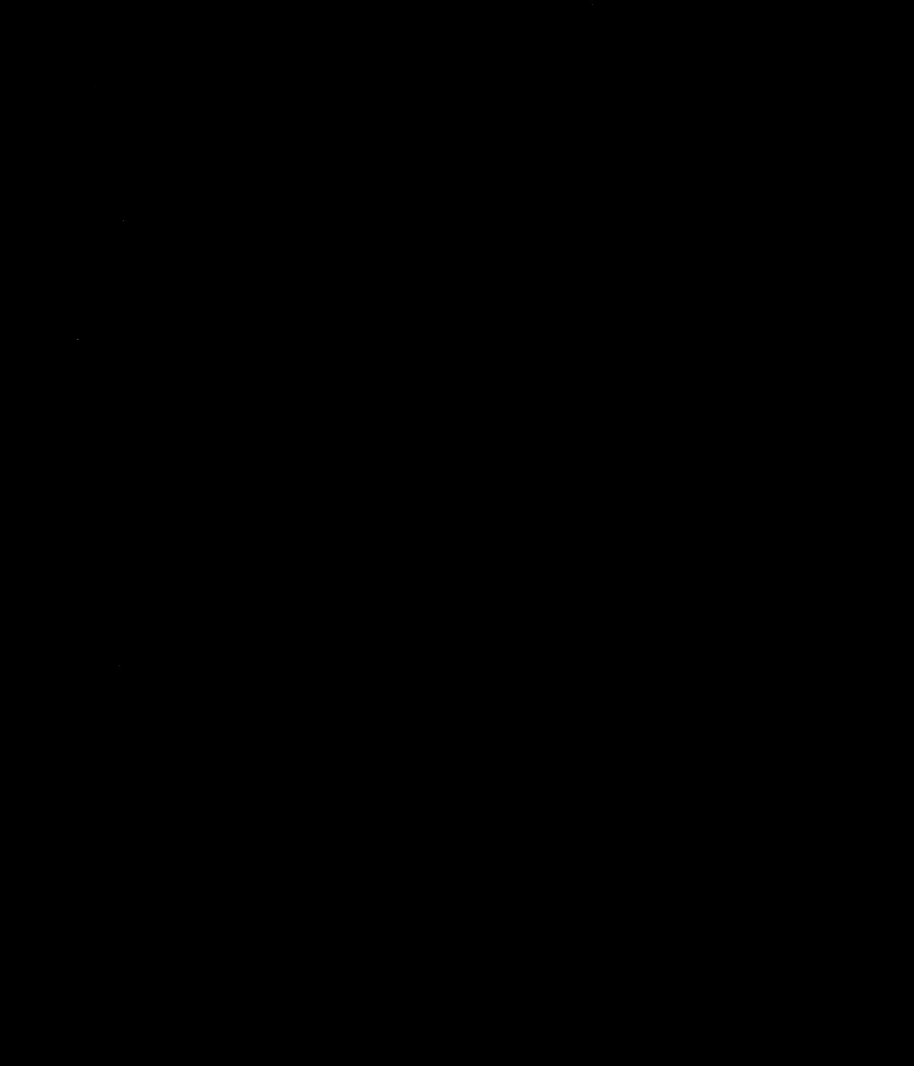

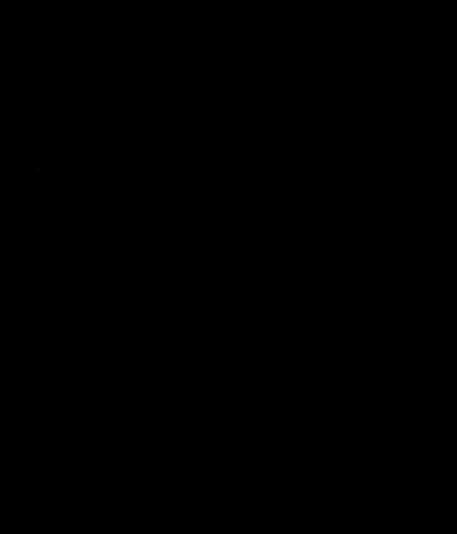

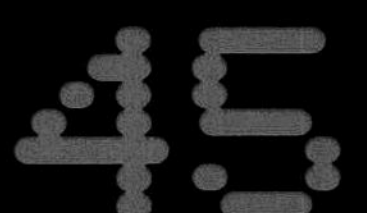

Fabien Barthez

Barthez looks to the heaven
joy and disbelief after Zida
heads his second goal from
corner, moments before th
whistle is blown for half tim

France v Brazil
3–0 (Final)
12 July 1998
Attendance 75,000
Stade de France
Paris, France

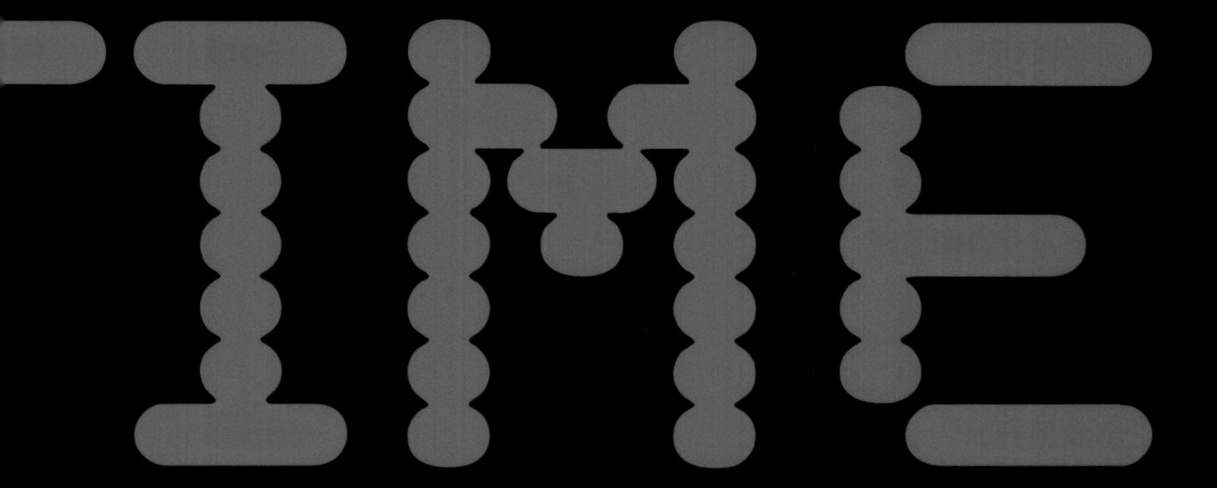
IME

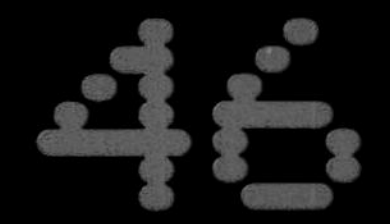

David Beckham

Referee Kim Milton Nielsen brandishes a red card to Beckham for his kick at Diego Simeone.

England v Argentina
2–2 AET (2nd round)
Argentina 4–3 on penalties
30 June 1998
Attendance 36,000
Stade Geoffroy-Guichard
Saint-Etienne, France

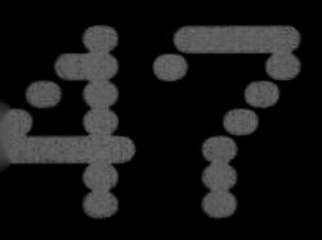

aul Gonzalez Blanco

Vith immaculate balance Raul cores an exquisite volley.

pain v Nigeria
–3 (Group stage)
3 June 1998
ttendance 33,257
tade de la Beaujoire
antes, France

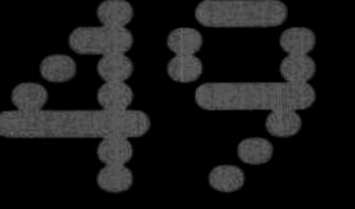

Ronaldo and Şenol Güneş

Ronaldo surges between four Turkish defenders and surprises Rüstü Reçber (the Turkish goalkeeper) with a 'toe poke' that finds the corner of the net. Güneş is worried about falling behind to the favourites.

Brazil v Turkey
1–0 (Semi-final)
26 June 2002
Attendance 61,058
Saitama Stadium
Saitama, Japan

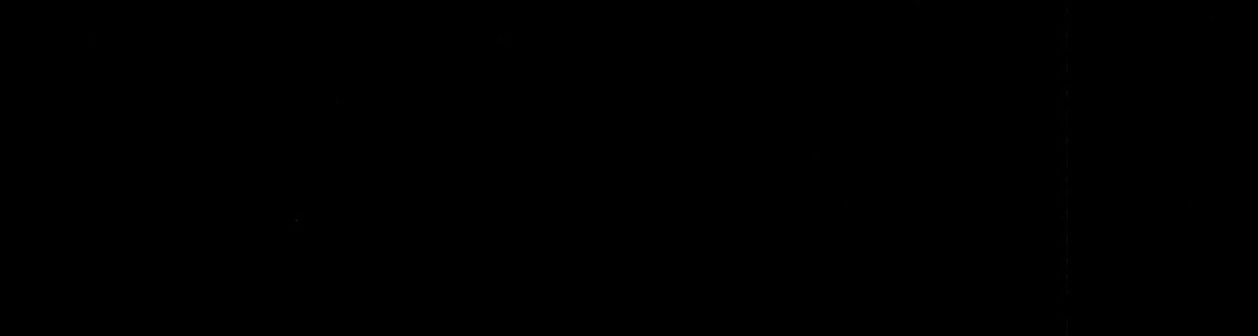

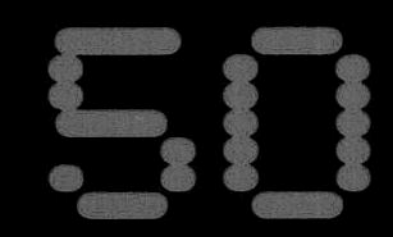

The hand of God

Maradona rises to a loose ball and uses his hand to beat the advancing Peter Shilton. He says it was “the hand of God”, perhaps an oblique reference, in his mind, to the injustice of the outcome of the Falklands war.

Argentina v England
2–1 (Quarter-final)
22 June 1986
Attendance 114,580
Estadio Azteca
Mexico City, Mexico

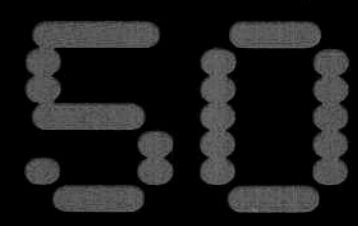

Harald Schumacher and Patrick Battiston

The fast-moving Schumacher ignores the ball and brutally floors Battiston in a dreadful foul that goes unpunished. Battiston is stretchered off. To add insult to injury, Schumacher saves the decisive penalty in the shoot-out that sees West Germany go through.

West Germany v France
3–3 AET (Semi-final)
West Germany 5–4 on penalties
8 July 1982
Attendance 71,000
Estadio Sánchez Pizjuán
Seville, Spain

54

Diego Maradona

Maradona collect
in his own half. H
away from Peter R
inside Terry Butch
Terry Fenwick, the
the ball past Shilt
the greatest indiv
ever scored.

Argentina v Engla
2–1 (Quarter-fina
22 June 1986
Attendance 114,5
Estadio Azteca
Mexico City, Mexi

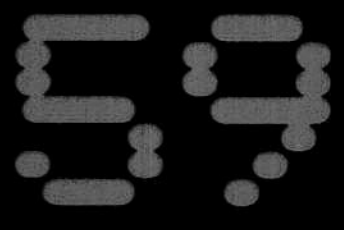

Pelé
With outrageous skill, Pelé volleys a Uruguayan goal kick straight back at the keeper from almost halfway. He's frustrated his shot is saved.

Brazil v Uruguay
3–1 (Semi-final)
17 June 1970
Attendance 51,261
Estadio Jalisco
Guadalajara, Mexico

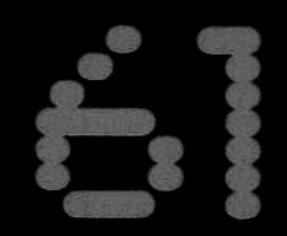

Rivelino

Rivelino's teammate stands in the East German wall. He ducks just as Rivelino strikes the ball. It fizzes through the gap and into the goal.

Brazil v East Germany
1–0 (Group stage)
26 June 1974
Attendance 58,463
Niedersachsenstadion
Hanover, West Germany

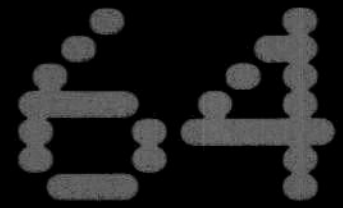

Nelinho

Isolated on the right wing, Nelinho bends his magnificent shot around Zoff and into the top corner with the outside of his right foot.

Brazil v Italy
2–1 (3rd place play-off)
24 June 1978
Attendance 69,659
Monumental
Buenos Aires, Argentina

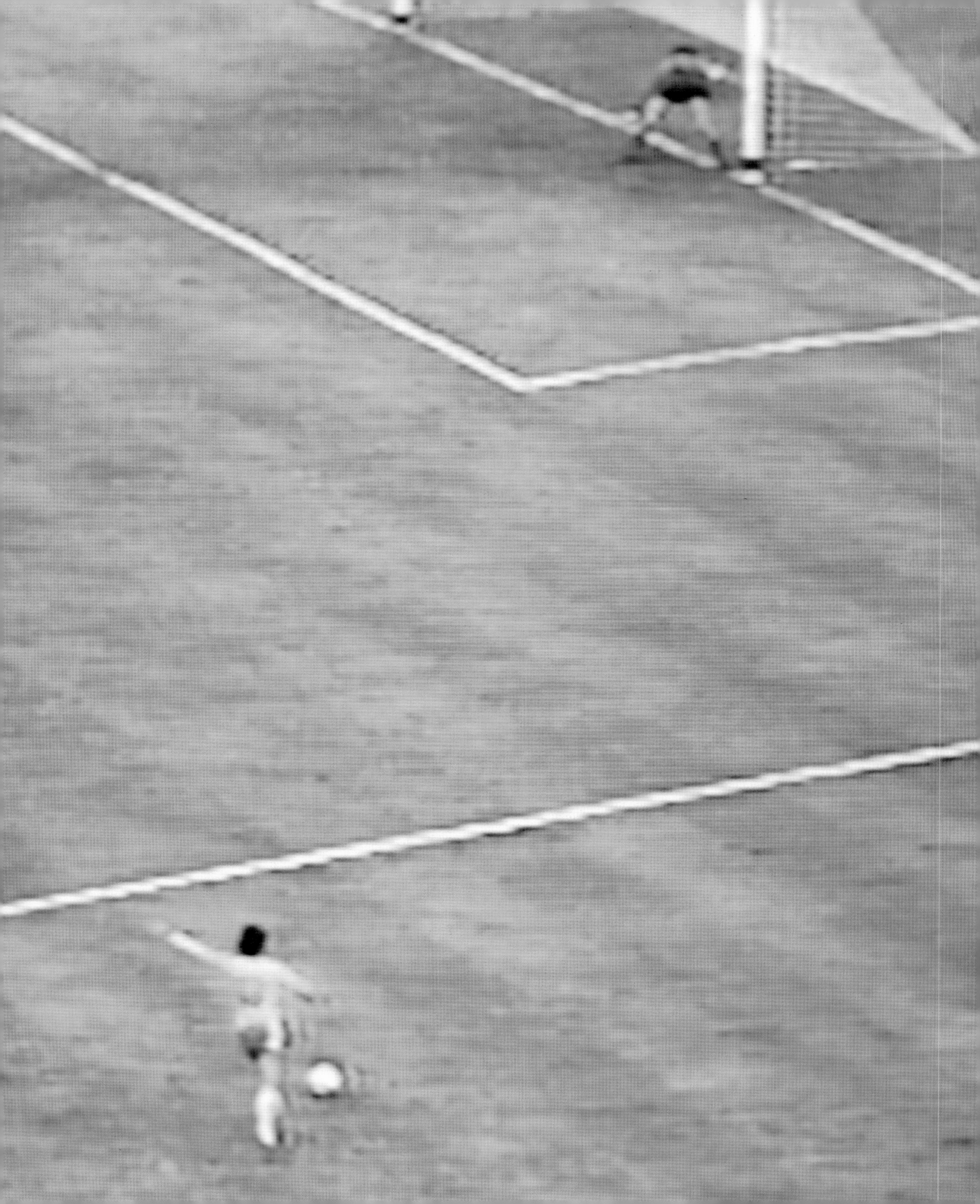

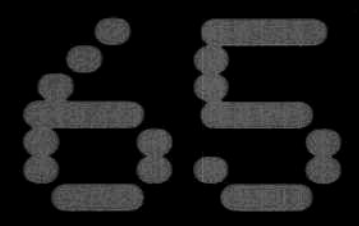

The Dutch team

The whole team celebrate their certain passage to the final after Cruijff's side-footed volley.

Holland v Brazil
2–0 (2nd round)
3 July 1974
Attendance 52,500
Westfalenstadion
Dortmund, West Germany

6

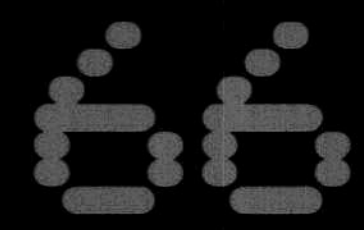

François Omam-Biyik
Omam-Biyik can hardly believe he's put Cameroon ahead against the reigning champions in the opening game of Italia '90.

Cameroon v Argentina
1–0 (Group stage)
8 June 1990
Attendance 73,780
San Siro
Milan, Italy

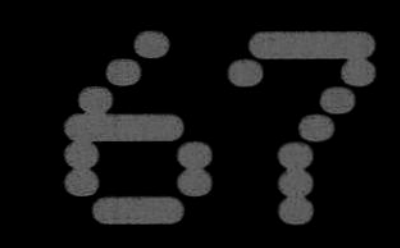

Oliver Kahn

Kahn, the best player of the tournament, makes his one and only mistake in spilling Rivaldo's shot. Ronaldo pounces: cruel.

Germany v Brazil
0–2 (Final)
30 June 2002
Attendance 69,029
Yokohama International Stadium
Yokohama, Japan

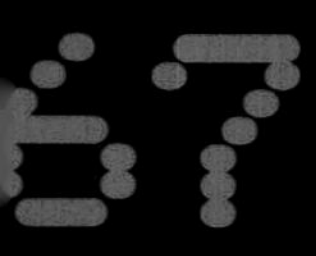

lichel Platini

latini is denied a legitimate qualizer by an erroneous ffside flag. West Germany o to the final for the second, uccessive time versus Platini nd France.

rance v West Germany
–2 (Semi-final)
5 June 1986
ttendance 47,500
stadio Jalisco
uadalajara, Mexico

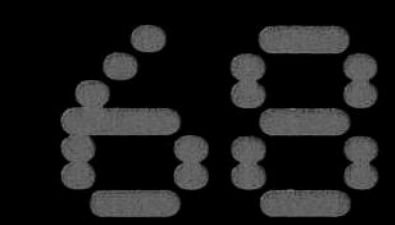

Santos Iriarte
Iriarte's shot leaves Argentina's goalkeeper, Botasso, helpless as Uruguay take a 3–2 lead.

Uruguay v Argentina
4–2 (Final)
30 July 1930
Attendance 68,346
Estadio Centenario
Montevideo, Uruguay

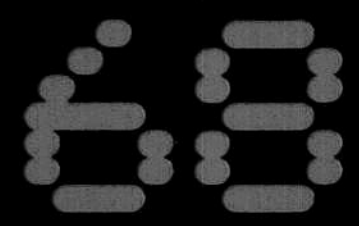

Archie Gemmill
Gemmill singlehandedly dismantles the Dutch defence, beats Jongbloed, and scores a brilliant individual goal. He can't, however, prevent Scotland's exit from the tournament on goal difference.

Scotland v Holland
3–2 (Group stage)
11 June 1978
Attendance 35,130
General San Martin Park
Mendoza, Argentina

15

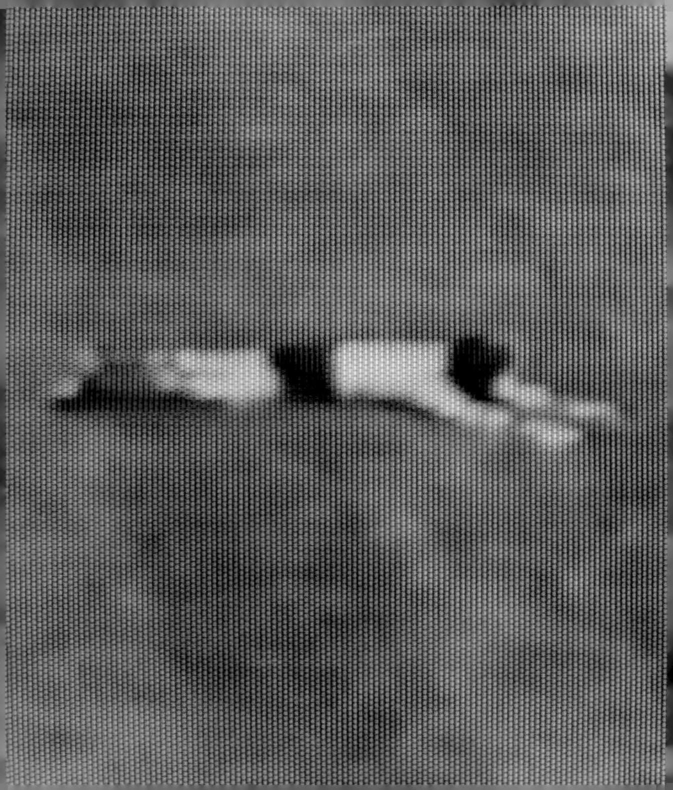

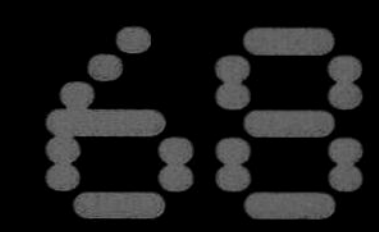

Enrico Albertosi

At full stretch, Albertosi fails to stop Gerson's rifleshot and is left face down, bereft.

Italy v Brazil
1–4 (Final)
21 June 1970
Attendance 107,412
Estadio Azteca
Mexico City, Mexico

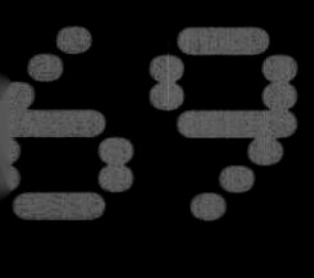

arco Tardelli

fter striking Italy's second goal,
n ecstatic Tardelli runs a joyous
rc around the Bernabéu.

aly v West Germany
–1 (Final)
1 July 1982
ttendance 90,089
stadio Santiago Bernabéu
adrid, Spain

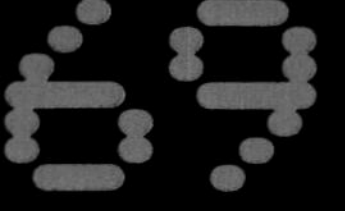

Franz Beckenbauer and Peter Bonetti

With West Germany 2–0 down, Beckenbauer storms past Mullery and shoots from twenty yards. The ball passes a retreating Bobby Moore and squirms under the body of Bonetti. Germany go on to win 3–2 in extra time.

West Germany v England
3–2 AET (Quarter-final)
14 June 1970
Attendance 32,000
Guanajuato
León, Mexico

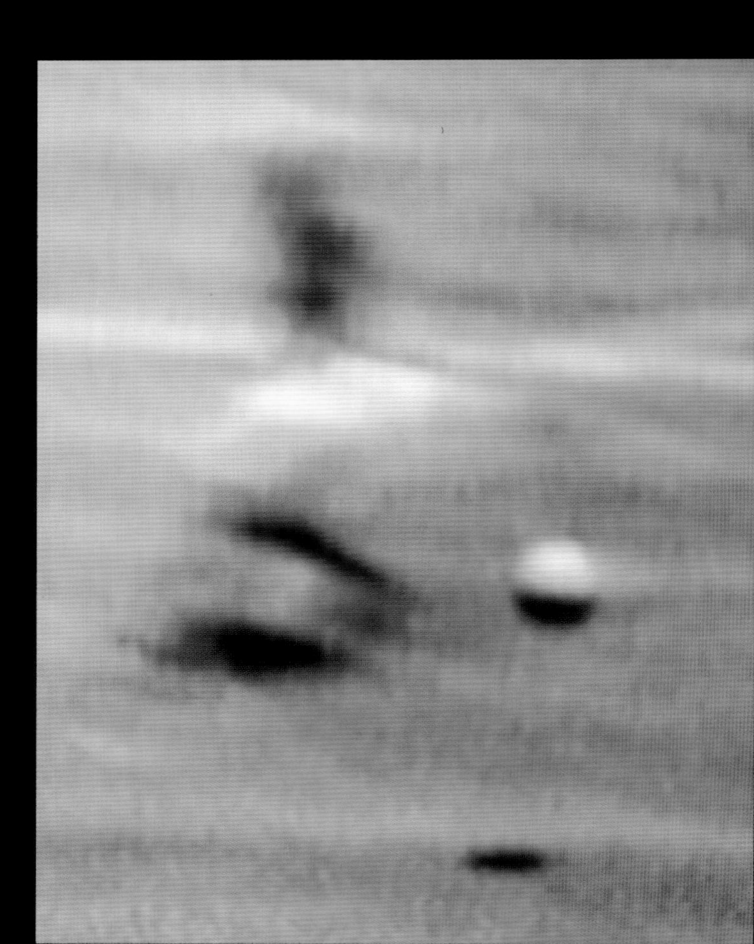

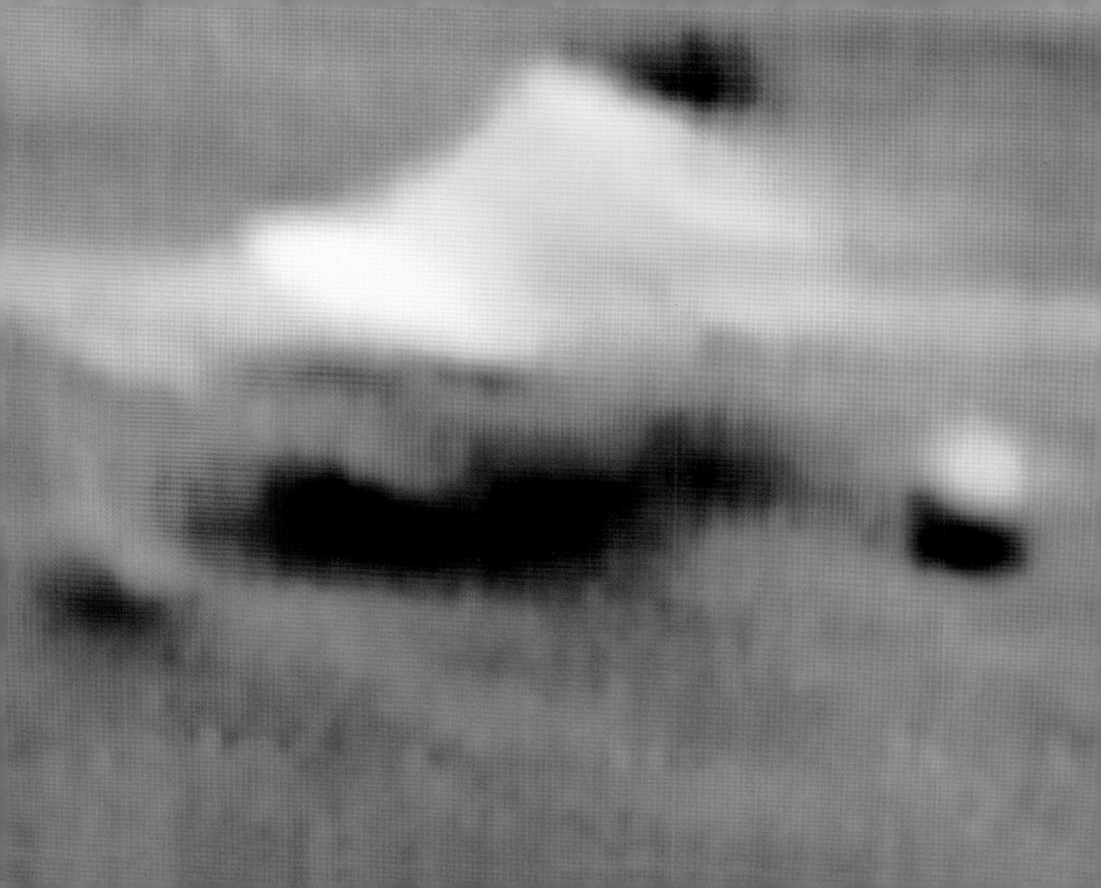

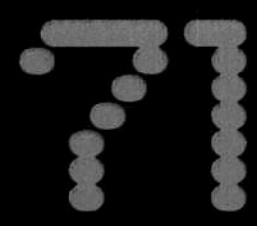

Ruud Gullit

Gullit is foiled by the German goalkeeper, Illgner, and Germany hang on. The Dutch team (winners of Euro 1988) of Gullit, Rijkaard and Van Basten are knocked out.

Holland v Germany
1–2 (2nd round)
24 June 1990
Attendance 74,559
San Siro
Milan, Italy

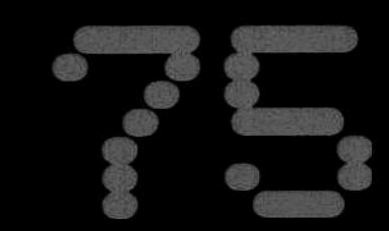

Michael Ballack

Ballack, having just been given a yellow card that would rule him out of the final, runs half the length of the pitch to score a most selfless goal.

Germany v South Korea
1–0 (Semi-final)
26 June 2002
Attendance 65,625
Seoul World Cup Stadium
Seoul, South Korea

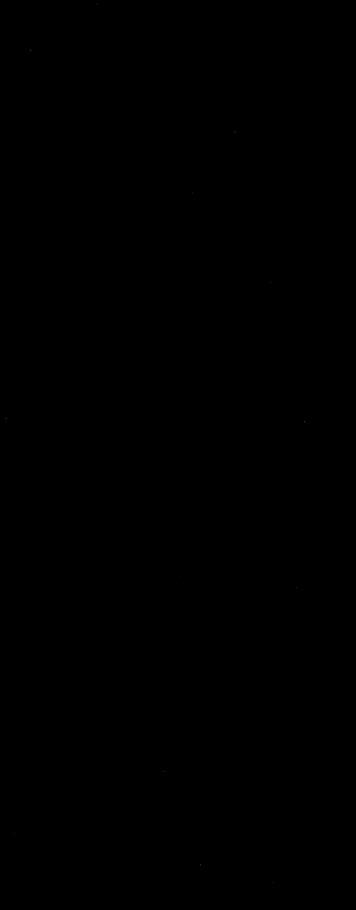

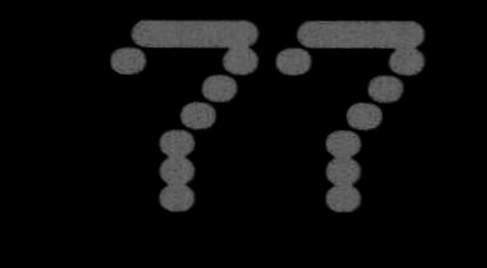

Viliam Schrojf

At 1–2 down, with the Czechs playing well, Schrojf, their goalkeeper, misjudges a cross in the sun that Vavá taps in to seal Brazil's second championship.

Czechoslovakia v Brazil
1–3 (Final)
17 June 1962
Attendance 68,679
Estadio Nacional
Santiago, Chile

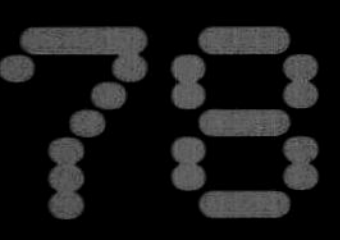

Yordan Letchkov

Letchkov scores a memorable diving header with his bald pate to take Bulgaria to their only semi-final.

Bulgaria v Germany
2–1 (Quarter-final)
10 July 1994
Attendance 72,416
Giants Stadium
East Rutherford, USA

LETCHKOV

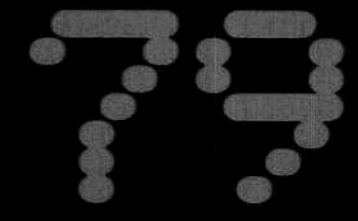

Amadeo Carrizo
Helmut Rahn hits a vicious swerving shot that Carrizo can do nothing to stop.

Argentina v West Germany
1–3 (Group stage)
8 June 1958
Attendance 31,156
Malmö Stadion
Malmö, Sweden

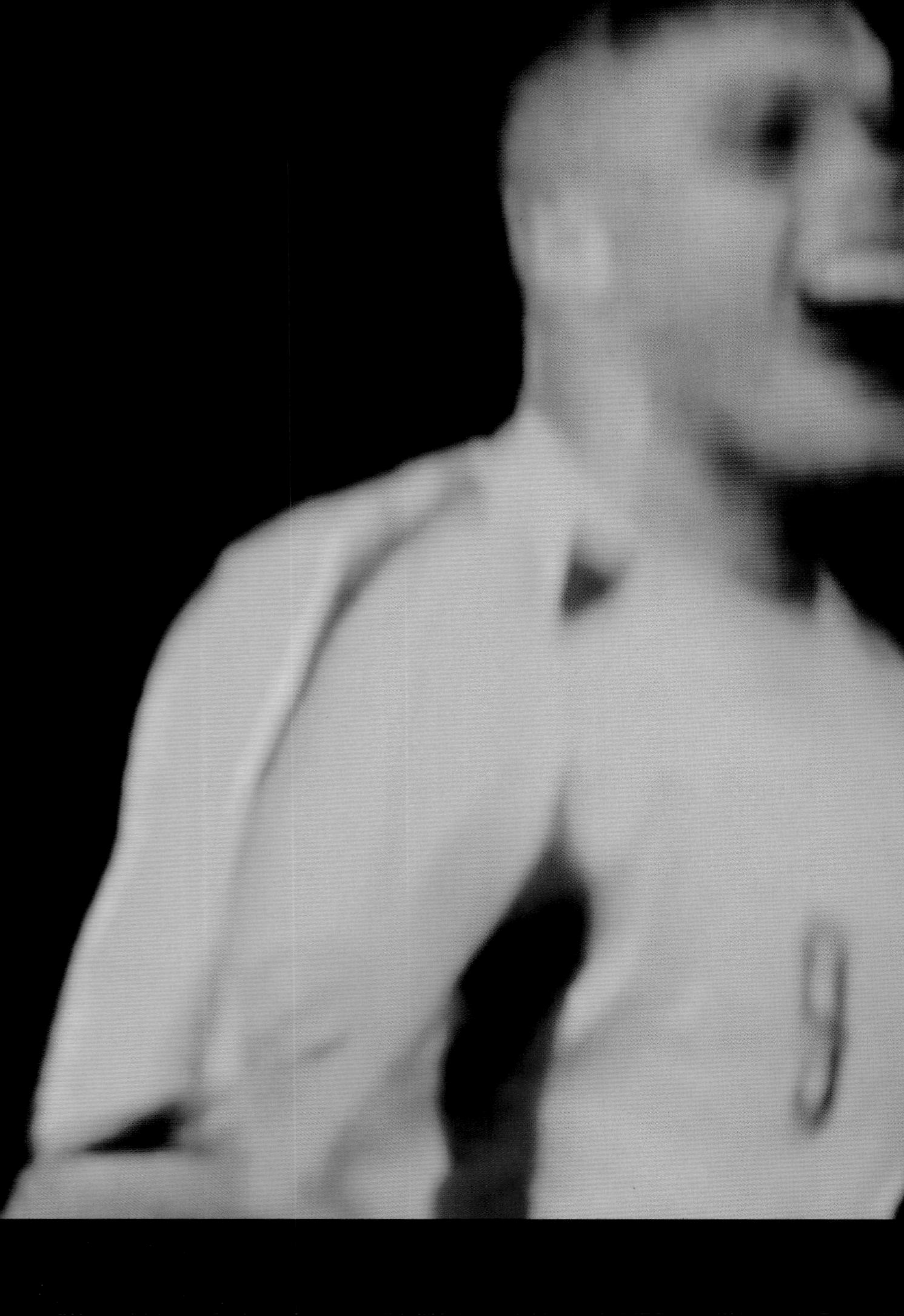

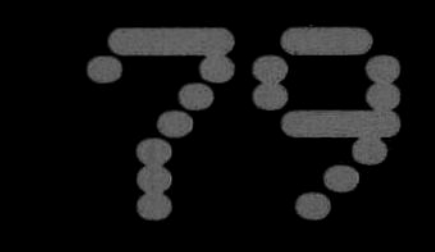

Ronaldo

Ronaldo scores his second goal to seal Brazil's victory in the final of 2002.

Brazil v Germany
2–0 (Final)
30 June 2002
Attendance 69,029
Yokohama International Stadium
Yokohama, Japan

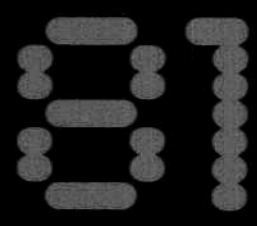

Sergio Goycochea
In the most cynical final in history, Goycochea is beaten by Brehme's penalty, which resulted from questionable contact in the area.

Argentina v West Germany
0–1 (Final)
8 July 1990
Attendance 73,603
Stadio Olimpico
Rome, Italy

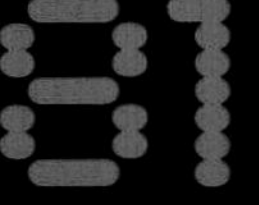

Alcide Ghiggia and Moacyr Barbosa

Ghiggia surges down the right wing and beats Barbosa at his near post in a match Brazil needed only to draw. Uruguay win the World Cup. Barbosa is blamed for the loss to their fierce rivals. The game is watched by more spectators than any before or since, as supporters surged through the stadium gates.

Uruguay v Brazil
2–1 (Final)
16 July 1950
Attendance 199,854
Maracaná
Rio de Janeiro, Brazil

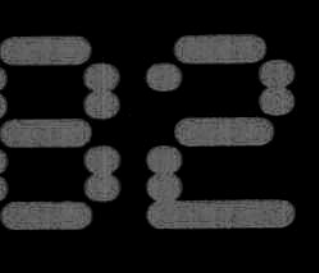

epp Maier

aier pulls off a fantastic
nger-tip save to prevent
oland equalizing late
 the game.

Vest Germany v Poland
–0 (2nd round)
 July 1974
ttendance 61,249
Valdstadion
rankfurt, West Germany

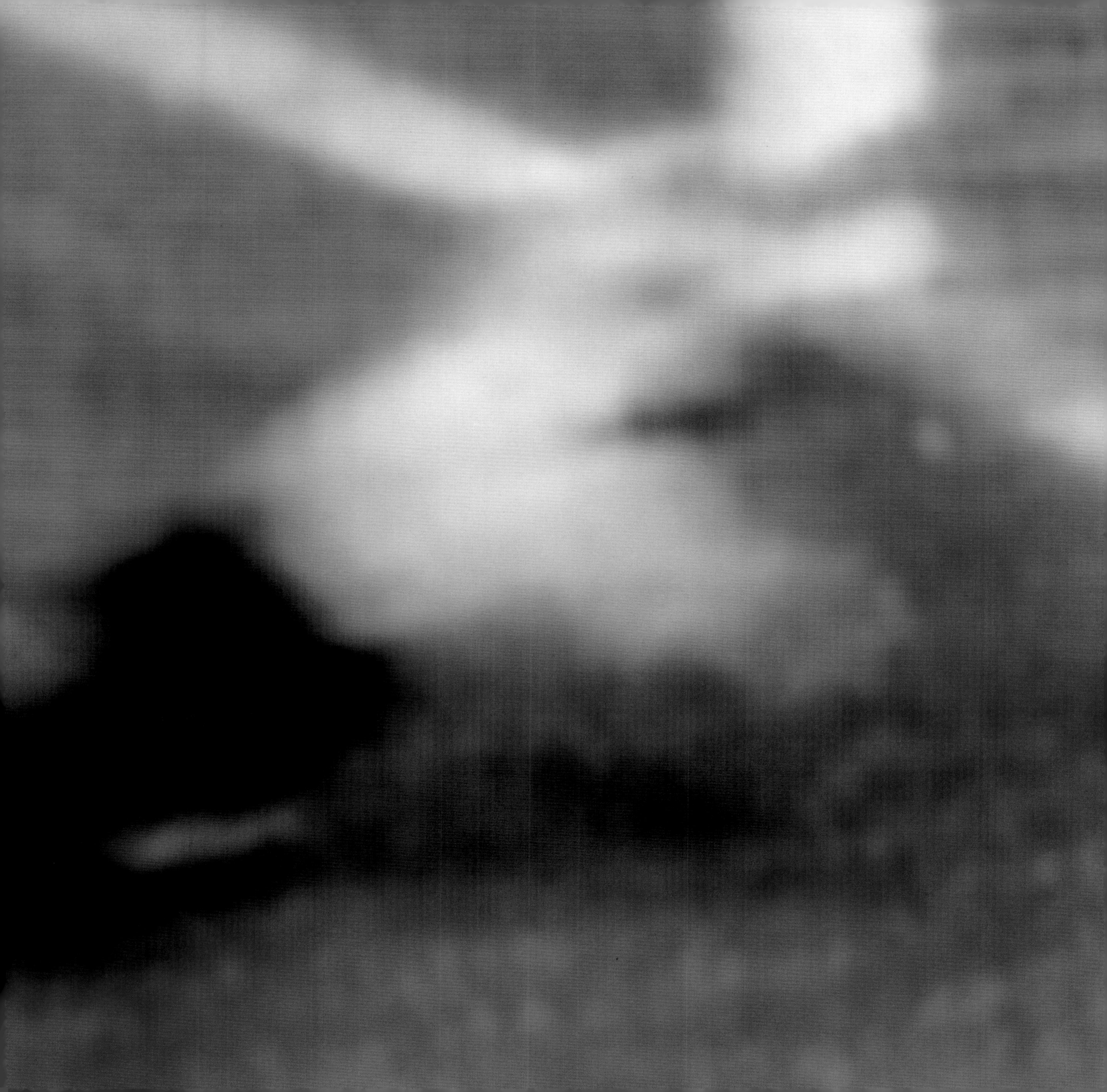

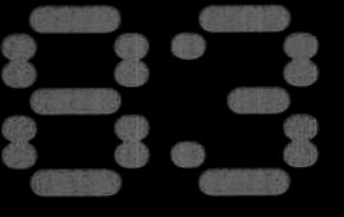

Harald Schumacher and Jorge Burruchaga

At 2–2, Burruchaga races on to a beautiful pass by Maradona and slides the ball under Schumacher.

Argentina v West Germany
3–2 (Final)
29 June 1986
Attendance 114,850
Estadio Azteca
Mexico City, Mexico

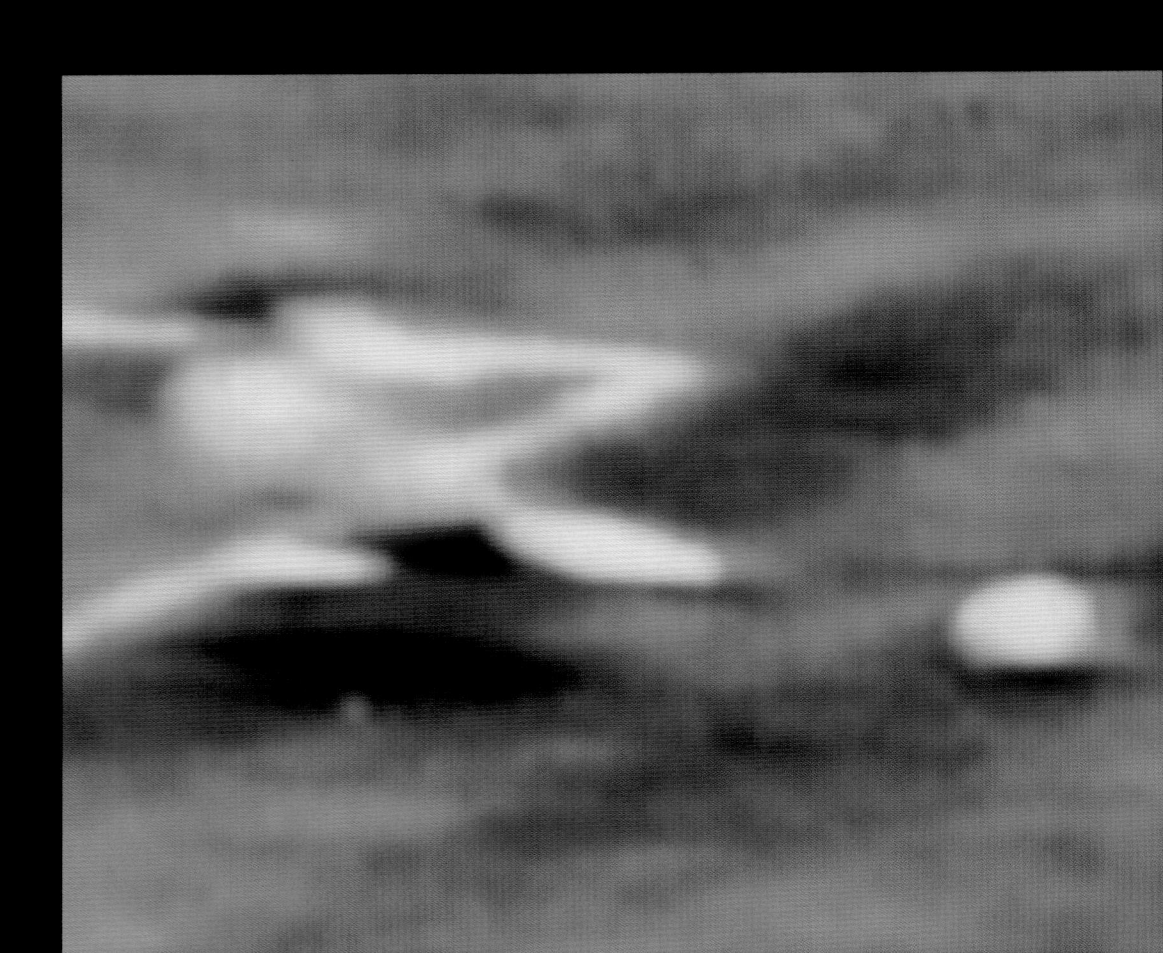

3
10

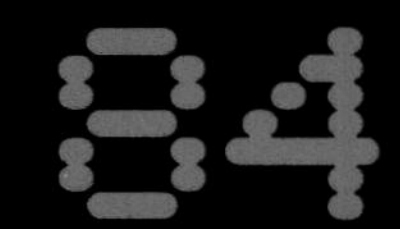

The Miracle of Bern

Helmut Rahn latches on to a poor Hungarian clearance and scores the winner that stuns the footballing world. Puskás's Magyars, unbeaten for three years, are finally defeated. The whole German team celebrates.

West Germany v Hungary
3–2 (Final)
4 July 1954
Attendance 62,472
Wankdorf Stadion
Bern, Switzerland

85

Eusébio

Eusébio runs to celebrate his second and Portugal's third goal in their convincing win over the holders.

Portugal v Brazil
3–1 (Group stage)
19 July 1966
Attendance 58,479
Goodison Park
Liverpool, England

13

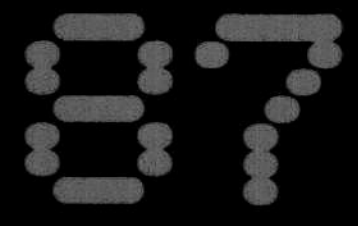

Rivaldo

Rivaldo, who has just deceived the referee and had a Turkish player sent off, lines up a penalty.

Brazil v Turkey
2–1 (Group stage)
3 June 2002
Attendance 33,842
Ulsan Munsu Stadium
Ulsan, South Korea

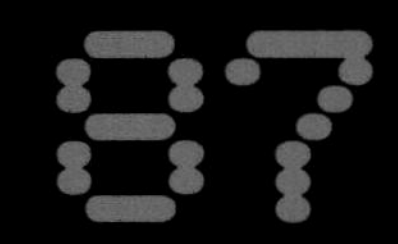

Carlos Alberto

After Clodoaldo has beaten two players with subtle feints, the ball is transferred down the right to Jairzinho, who squares the ball to Pelé. From Pelé's beautifully weighted side-foot pass Carlos Alberto smashes the ball into the bottom corner of the net: the best team goal ever scored.

Brazil v Italy
4–1 (Final)
21 June 1970
Attendance 107,412
Estadio Azteca
Mexico City, Mexico

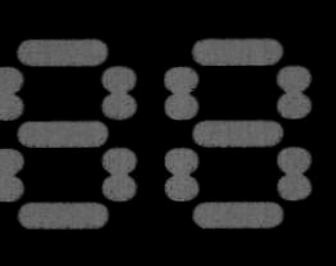

Pelé and Ladislao Mazurkiewicz

Pelé, in his pomp, dummies the goalkeeper before running behind him to collect Tostao's through ball.

Brazil v Uruguay
3–1 (Semi-final)
17 June 1970
Attendance 51,261
Estadio Jalisco
Guadalajara, Mexico

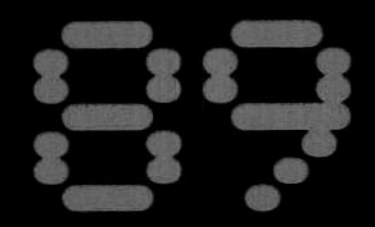

Christian Vieri

Vieri, with the goal at his mercy, but on his unfavoured right foot, misses from three yards.

Italy v South Korea
1–2 AET (2nd round)
18 June 2002
Attendance 38,588
Daejeon World Cup Stadium
Daejeon, South Korea

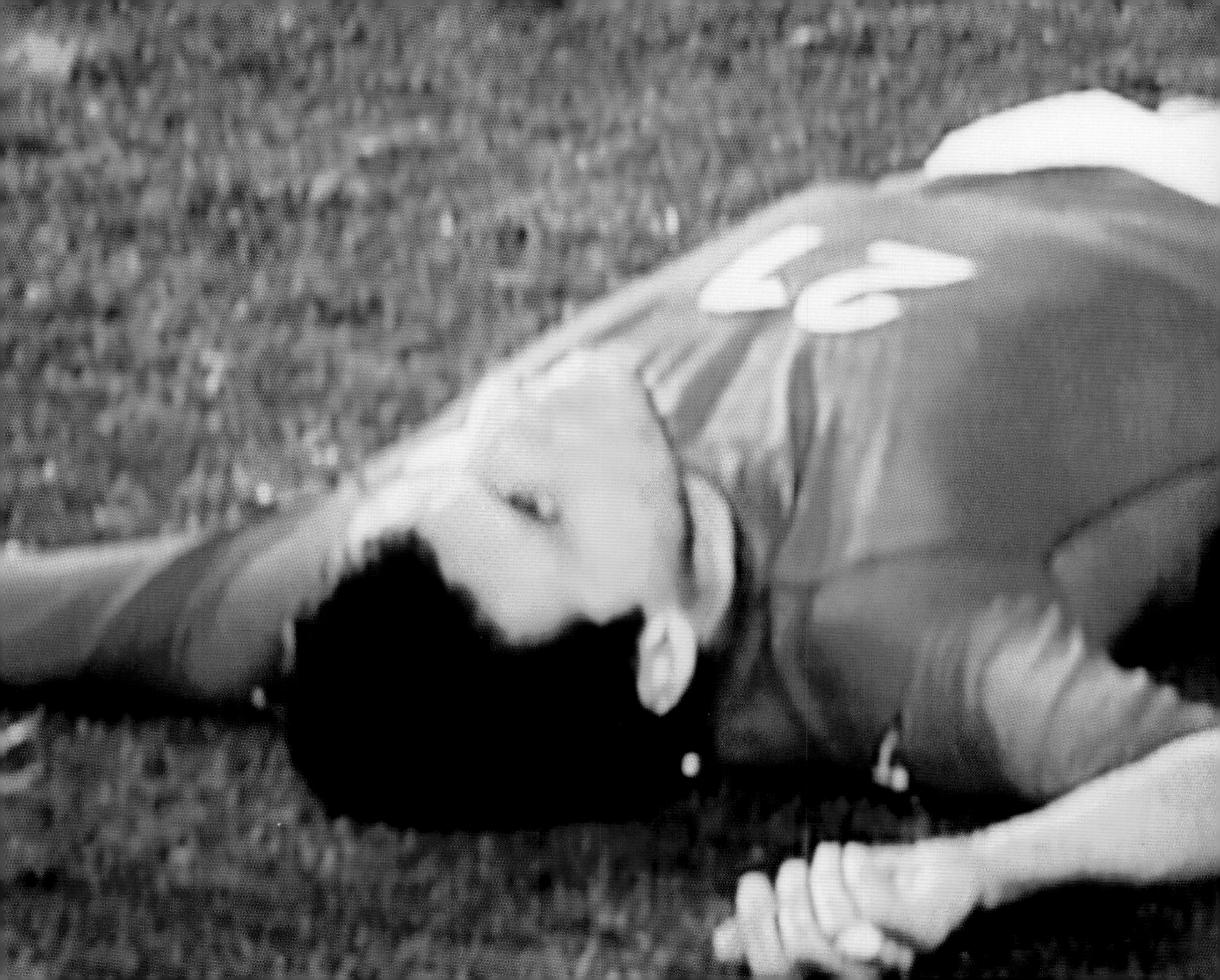

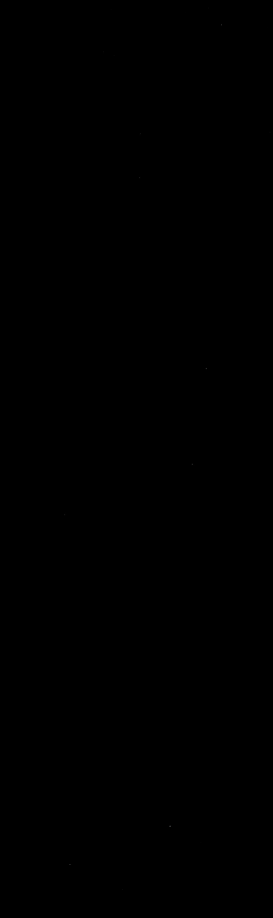

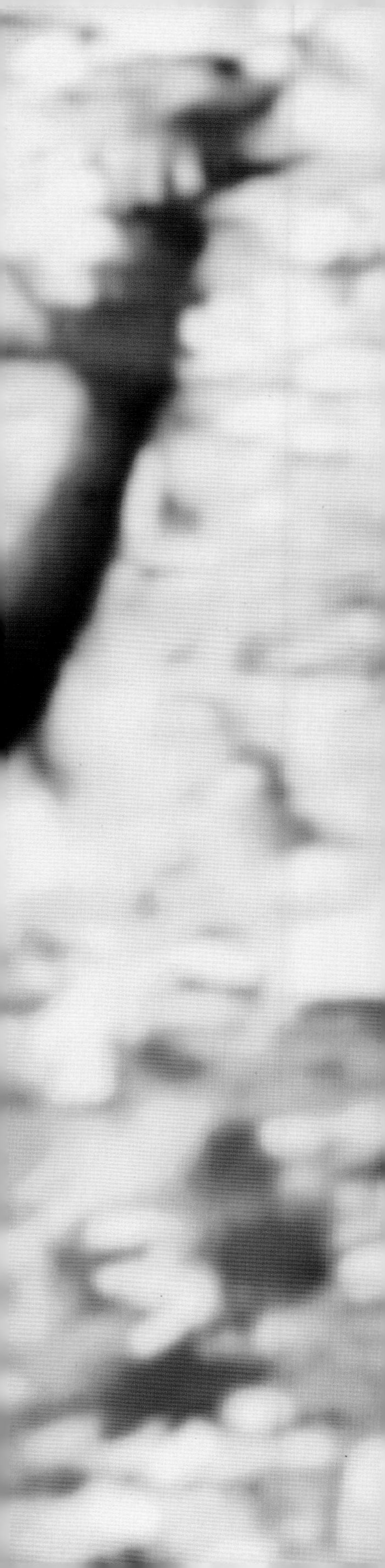

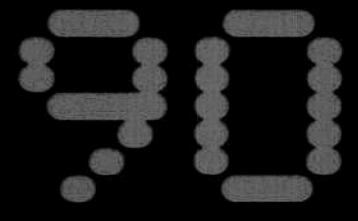

Clive Thomas
Brazil take a corner in the final seconds of the match. The ball is delivered and Zico scores with a header. Unfortunately, referee Thomas had blown the whistle while the ball was in flight and so he disallows the goal. The whole Brazilian team remonstrate with him. It's the last time he referees a World Cup game.

Brazil v Sweden
1–1 (Group stage)
3 June 1978
Attendance 38,618
Estadio José Maria Minella
Mar del Plata, Argentina

EXTRA TIME

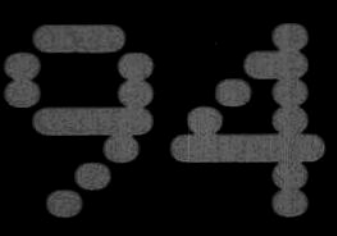

İlhan Mansiz

Running to the near post, Mansiz hits a delightful half-volley to score the 'golden goal' that takes Turkey into the semi-finals.

Turkey v Senegal
1–0 AET (Quarter-final)
22 June 2002
Attendance 44,233
Nagai Stadium
Osaka, Japan

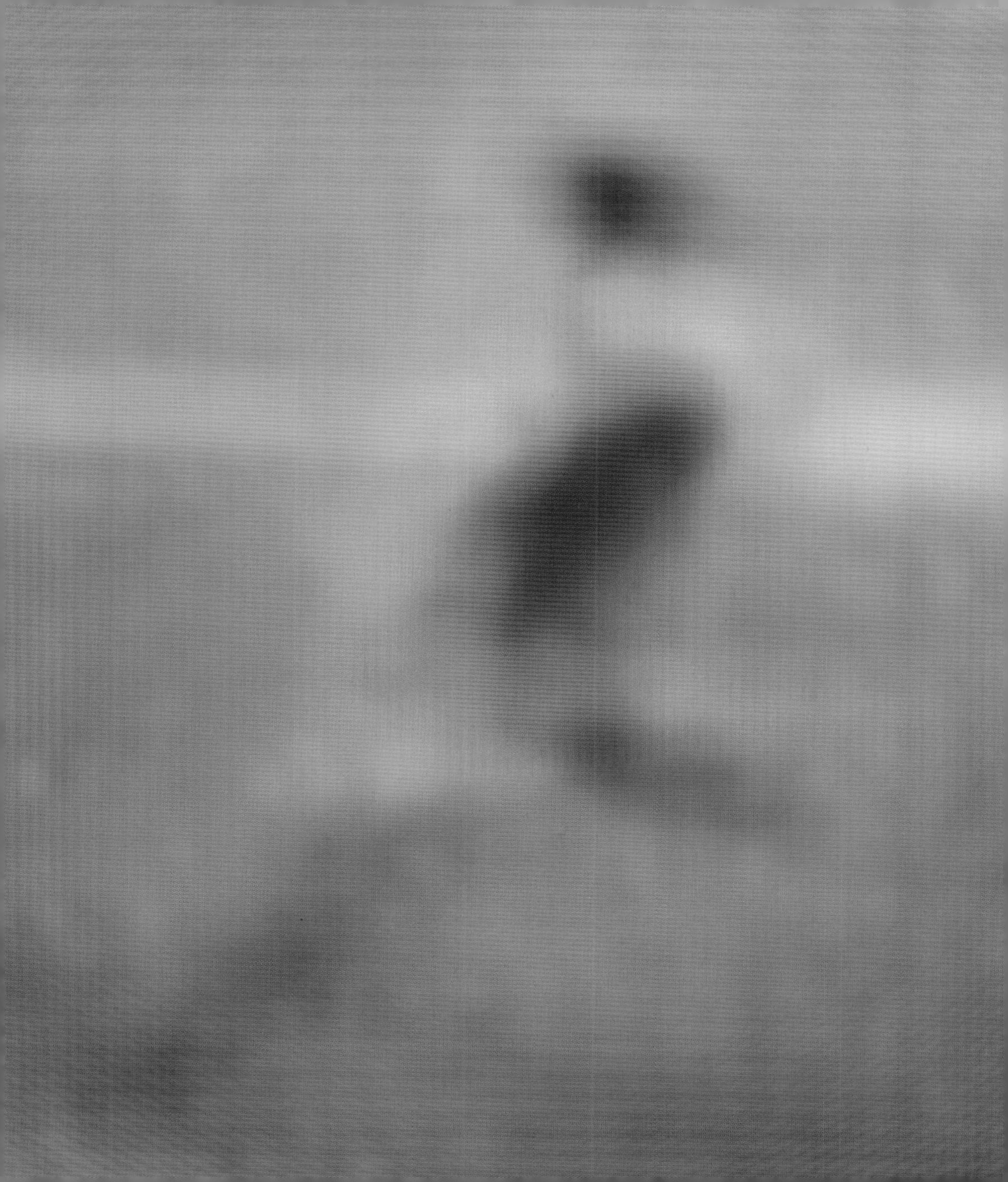

Bobby Charlton and Hans Tilkowski
The Russian linesman Bakhramov confirms to Swiss referee Dienst that Hurst's shot has crossed the line. Charlton is elated, Tilkowski crestfallen.

England v West Germany
4–2 AET (Final)
30 July 1966
Attendance 93,802
Wembley
London, England

114

Mario Kempes
The brilliant Kempes drifts between two Dutch defenders and bundles the ball over the line to give Argentina victory in Buenos Aires.

Argentina v Holland
3–1 AET (Final)
25 June 1978
Attendance 76,609
Monumental
Buenos Aires, Argentina

116

The French team

France are denied a penalty after an outrageous foul by Brazil's goalkeeper, Carlos, on Rocheteau. Platini, Tigana and Rocheteau are appalled.

France v Brazil
1–1 AET (Quarter-final)
France 4–3 on penalties
21 June 1986
Attendance 65,677
Estadio Jalisco
Guadalajara, Mexico

Ahn Jung-Hwan
Ahn heads the 'golden goal' three minutes before the end of extra time. He wheels away in delight as South Korea advance to the quarter-finals.

South Korea v Italy
2–1 AET (2nd round)
18 June 2002
Attendance 38,588
Daejeon World Cup Stadium
Daejeon, South Korea

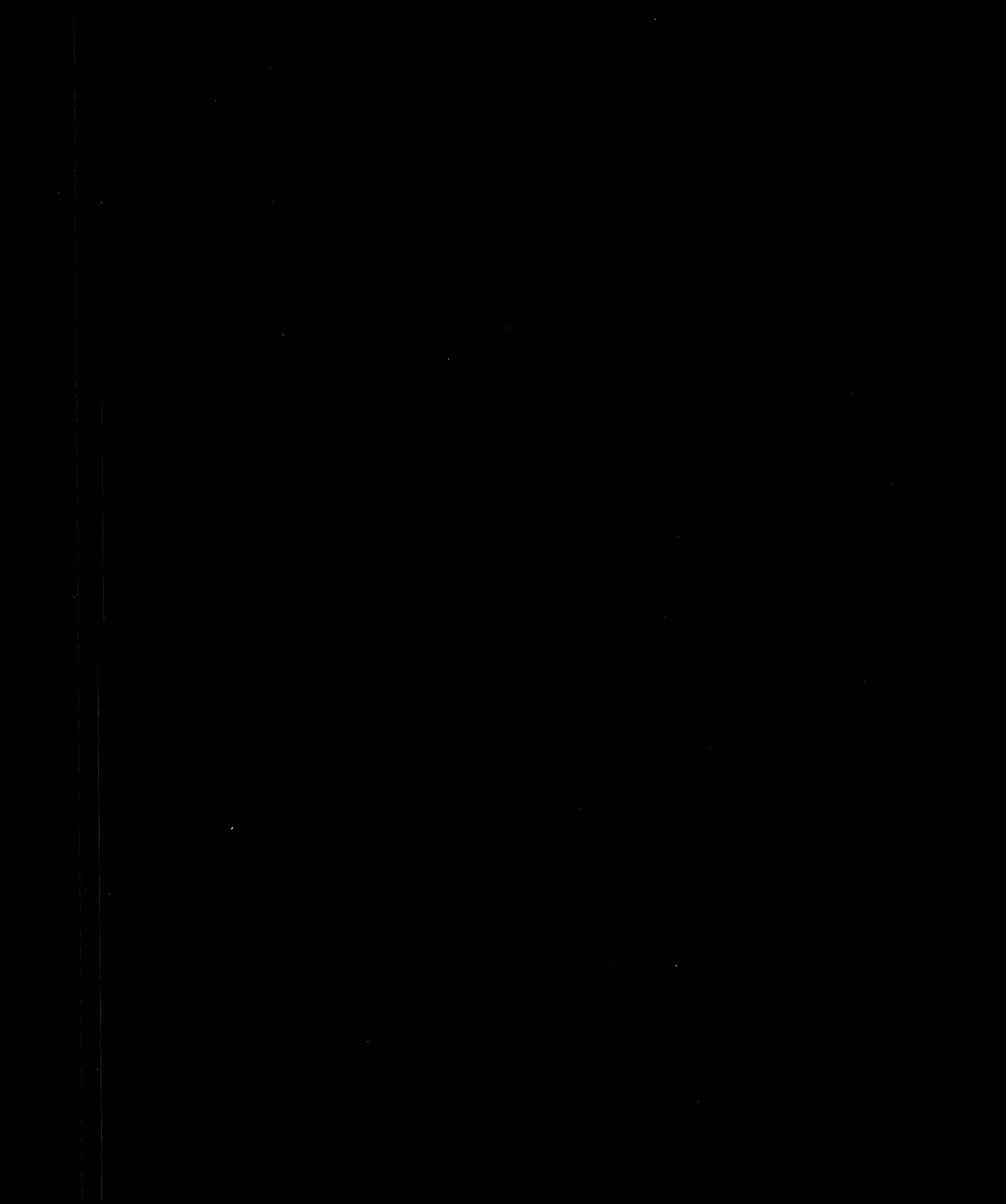

PENALTIES

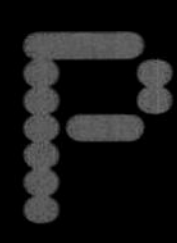

Roberto Baggio

Baggio, faced by Taffarel, balloons the tenth and final penalty over the bar. Italy lose.

Italy v Brazil
0–0 AET (Final)
Brazil 3–2 on penalties
17 July 1994
Attendance 94,194
Rose Bowl
Pasadena, USA

Luis Fernandez

Fernandez, crushed by the pressure, walks to take the decisive penalty against Brazil.

France v Brazil
1–1 AET (Quarter-final)
France 4–3 on penalties
21 June 1986
Attendance 65,677
Estadio Jalisco
Guadalajara, Mexico

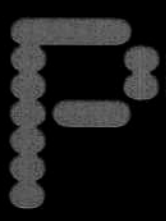

Stuart Pearce

Pearce misses the crucial penalty and retreats to the halfway line to be consoled by his teammates. Nothing can console him.

England v Germany
1–1 AET (Semi-final)
Germany 4–3 on penalties
4 July 1990
Attendance 62,628
Stadio delle Alpi
Turin, Italy

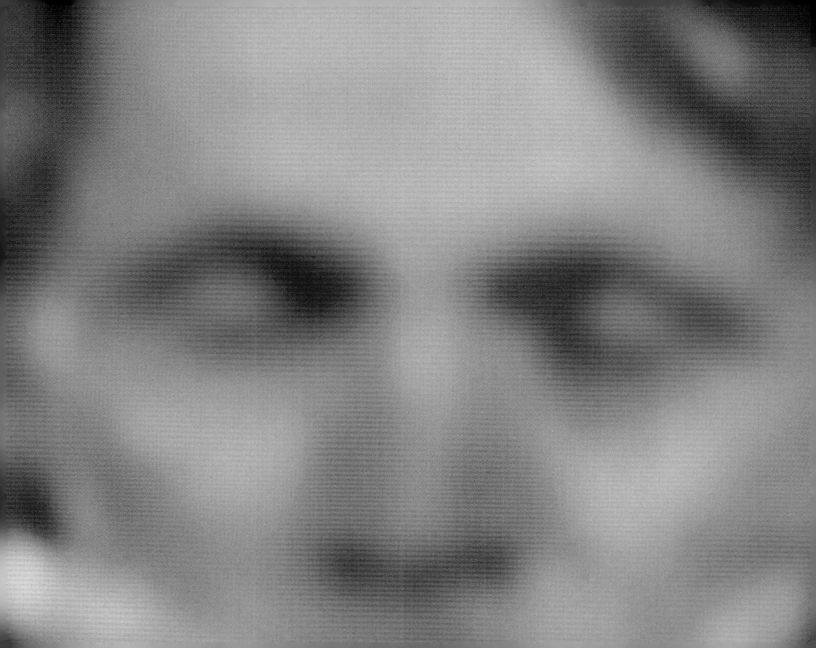

AFTER THE

FINAL WHISTLE

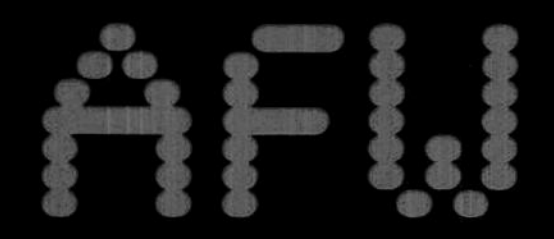

Jack Charlton
The final whistle is blown and a shattered Charlton takes a moment to reflect.

England v West Germany
4–2 AET (Final)
30 July 1966
Attendance 93,802
Wembley
London, England

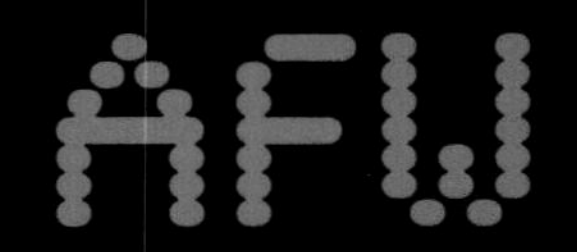

Pelé and Bobby Moore
Pelé and Moore show affection and respect in the wake of Brazil's victory.

Brazil v England
1–0 (Group stage)
7 June 1970
Attendance 70,950
Estadio Jalisco
Guadalajara, Mexico

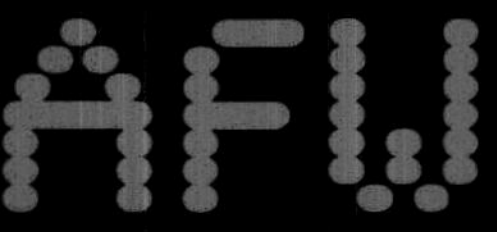

Pelé

After scoring two goals in the final, the seventeen-year-old Pelé is overcome by Brazil's victory.

Brazil v Sweden
5–2 (Final)
29 June 1958
Attendance 49,737
Råsunda Stadion
Stockholm, Sweden

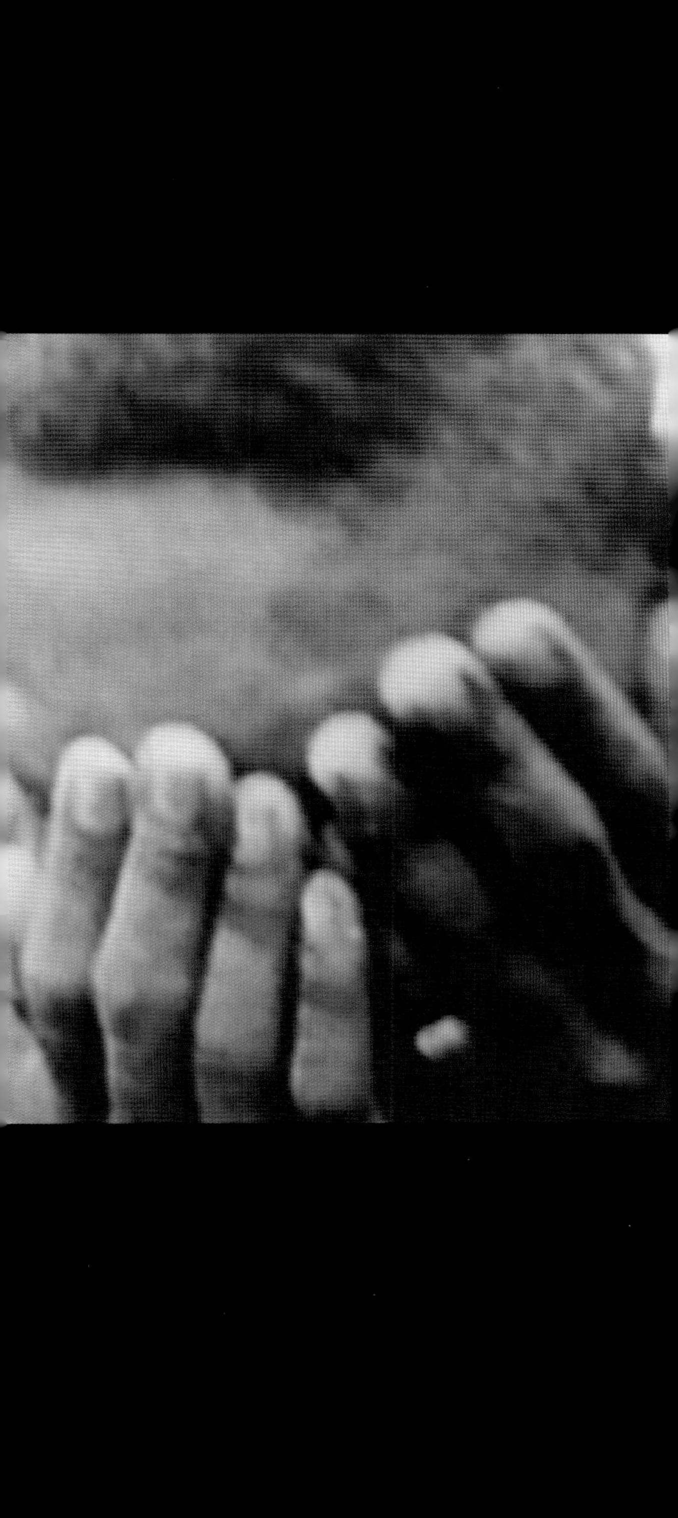

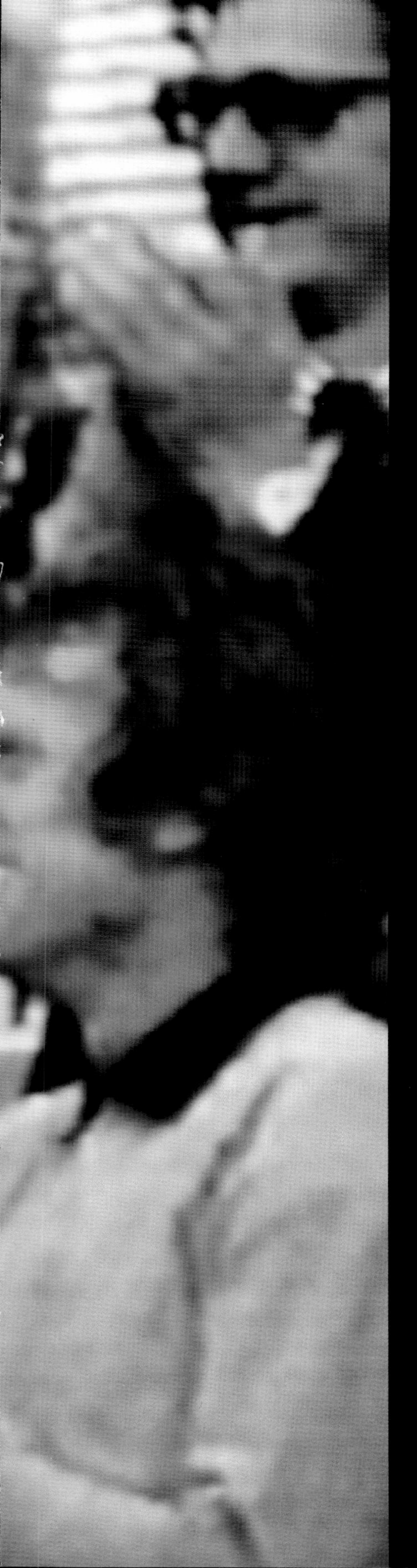

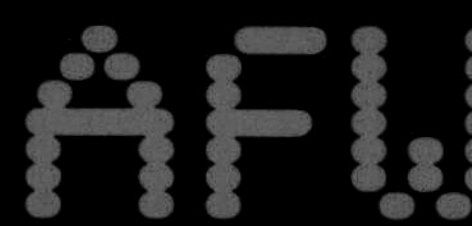

Franz Beckenbauer and Sepp Maier
Beckenbauer holds the troph
aloft in the company of Maie
The dignatories look on.

West Germany v Holland
2–1 (Final)
7 July 1974
Attendance 77,833
Olympiastadion
Munich, West Germany

RESULTS

The teams, in order of their overall success in World Cup tournaments.

Brazil

5 wins in
7 finals

02 Vavá

11 Rivelino

12 Socratés

14 Pelé

45 Ronaldinho

49 Ronaldo

59 Pelé

61 Rivelino

64 Nelinho

79 Ronaldo

81 Moacyr Barbosa

87 Rivaldo

87 Carlos Alberto

88 Pelé

90 Clive Thomas

AFW Pelé

AFW Pelé

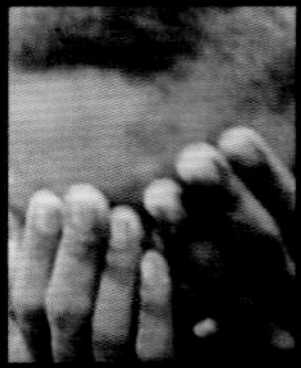

AFW Jules Rimet Trophy

Germany

3 wins in
7 finals

43 Gerd Müller

67 Oliver Kahn

69 Franz Beckenbauer

75 Michael Ballack

82 Sepp Maier

83 Harald Schumacher

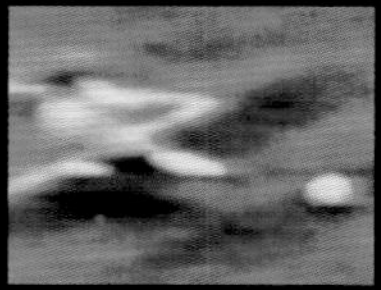

84 The Miracle of Bern

119 Hans Tilkowski

AFW Franz Beckenbauer

Italy

24 Paolo Rossi

24 Paolo Rossi

37 Roberto Boninsegna

68 Enrico Albertosi

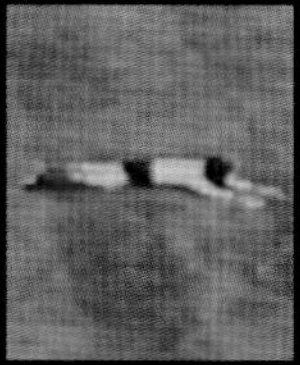

69 Marco Tardelli

89 Christian Vieri

P Roberto Baggio

3 wins in
5 finals

Argentina

50 The hand of God

54 Diego Maradona

79 Amadeo Carrizo

81 Sergio Goycochea

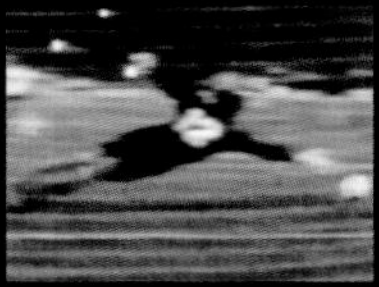

83 Jorge Burruchaga

114 Mario Kempes

2 wins in
4 finals

Uruguay

68 Santos Iriarte

81 Alcide Ghiggia

2 wins in
2 finals

France

14 Marcel Desailly

15 Just Fontaine

36 Zinédine Zidane

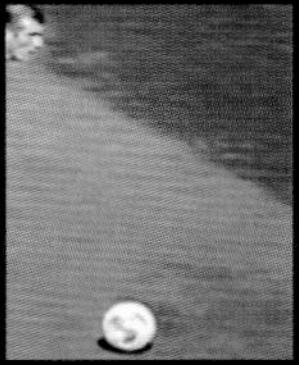

45 Fabien Barthez

1 win in 1 final
3 semi-finals

50 Patrick Battiston

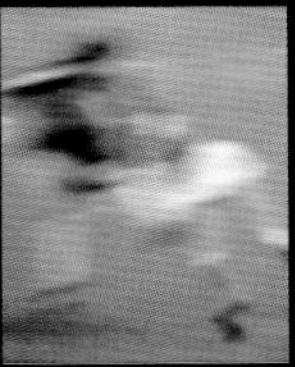

67 Michel Platini

70 Lilian Thuram

116 The French team

P Trézéguet and Henry

P Luis Fernandez

P Luis Fernandez

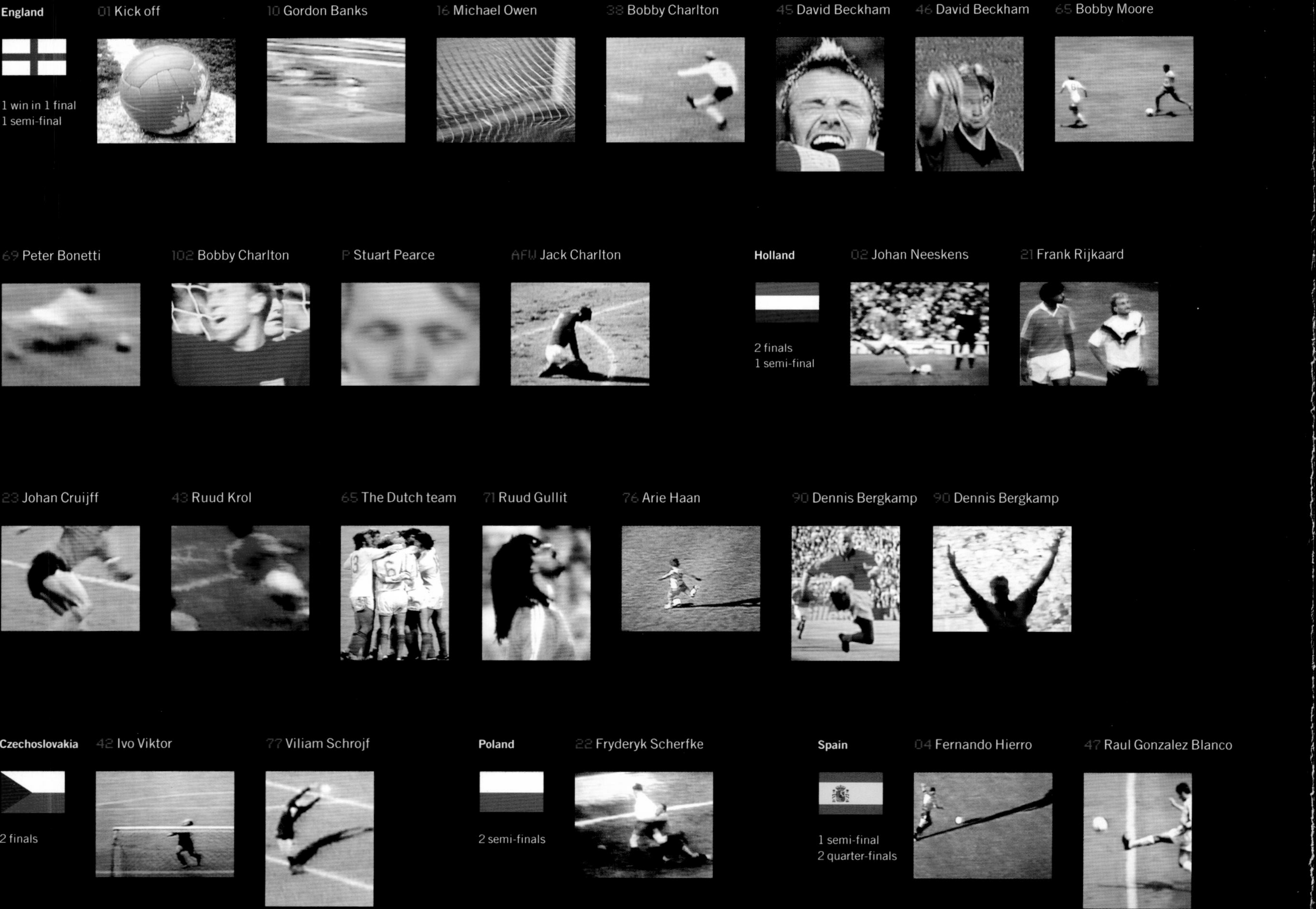
England
1 win in 1 final
1 semi-final
01 Kick off
10 Gordon Banks
16 Michael Owen
38 Bobby Charlton
45 David Beckham
46 David Beckham
65 Bobby Moore
69 Peter Bonetti
102 Bobby Charlton
P Stuart Pearce
AFW Jack Charlton
Holland
2 finals
1 semi-final
02 Johan Neeskens
21 Frank Rijkaard
23 Johan Cruijff
43 Ruud Krol
65 The Dutch team
71 Ruud Gullit
76 Arie Haan
90 Dennis Bergkamp
90 Dennis Bergkamp
Czechoslovakia
2 finals
42 Ivo Viktor
77 Viliam Schrojf
Poland
2 semi-finals
22 Fryderyk Scherfke
Spain
1 semi-final
2 quarter-finals
04 Fernando Hierro
47 Raul Gonzalez Blanco

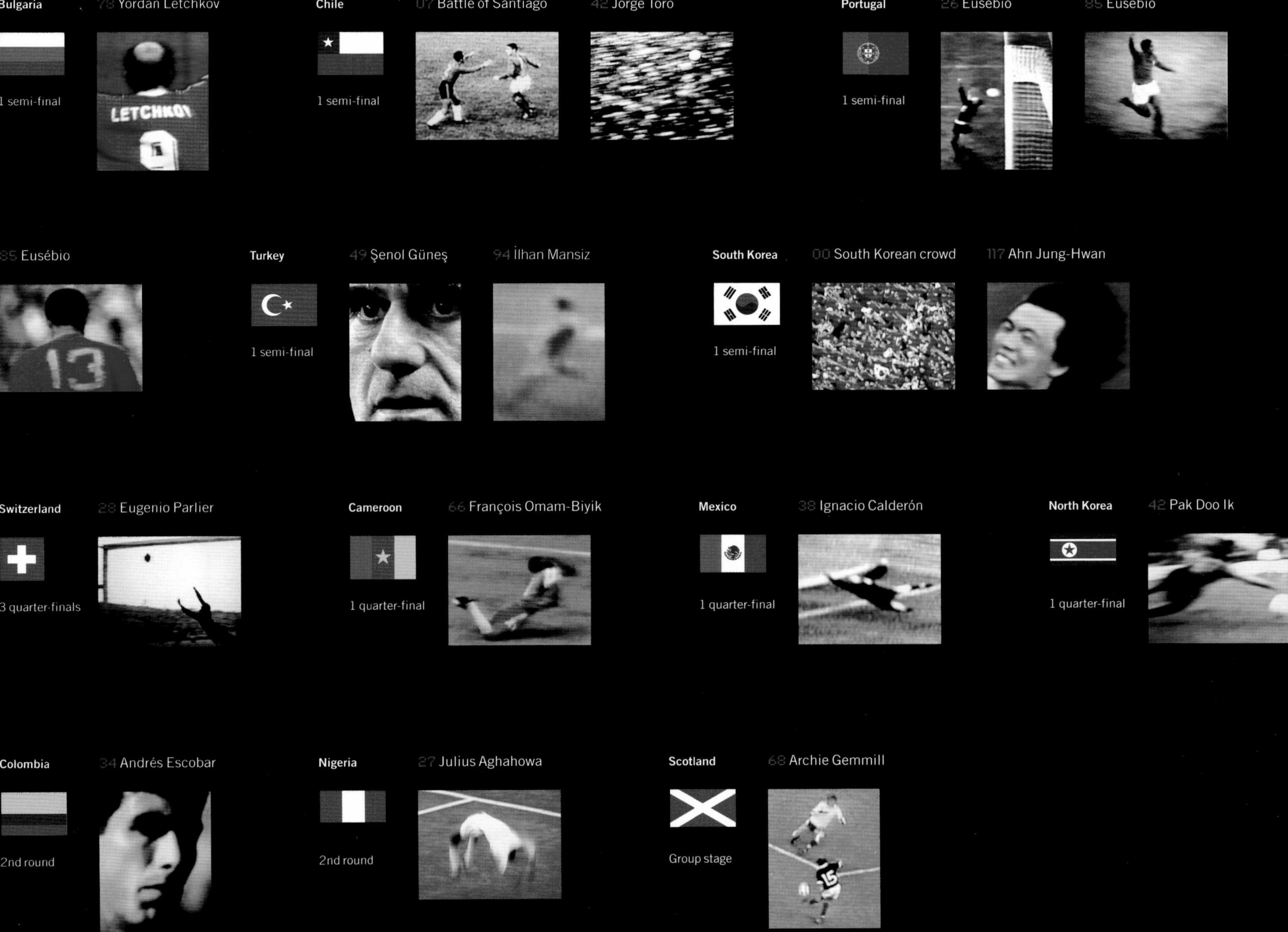
Bulgaria
78 Yordan Letchkov
1 semi-final
LETCHKOV
Chile
07 Battle of Santiago
42 Jorge Toro
1 semi-final
Portugal
26 Eusébio
85 Eusébio
1 semi-final
85 Eusébio
13
Turkey
49 Şenol Güneş
94 İlhan Mansiz
1 semi-final
South Korea
00 South Korean crowd
117 Ahn Jung-Hwan
1 semi-final
Switzerland
28 Eugenio Parlier
3 quarter-finals
Cameroon
66 François Omam-Biyik
1 quarter-final
Mexico
38 Ignacio Calderón
1 quarter-final
North Korea
42 Pak Doo Ik
1 quarter-final
Colombia
34 Andrés Escobar
2nd round
Nigeria
27 Julius Aghahowa
2nd round
Scotland
68 Archie Gemmill
Group stage
15

Acknowledgements

I should like to thank FIFA for their help and co-operation with this project.

I should like to thank the Association of Football Statisticians (and Mark Baber in particular), Guy Oliver, Dave Whelan and Cris Freddi for their statistical input, which has been invaluable.

I should also like to thank Giles and 'Football Phil' for their enthusiasm and help in realizing this book; David and Richard for their ideas and for making the whole thing possible; Ian and Tanya for their beautiful design and attention to detail; Mark F. for his introduction to Merrell Publishers and 'Hugh the haircut' for his vision and good faith; Nicola, Michelle, Anthea, Helen, Paul and Mrs Harmison for their hard work, repartee and amusement at my phone; Robin P., Addie, Thomas S., Ezequiel and Jennifer for their assistance; and the Kensington Turbo Mouse for his unlikely, but significant, contribution.

And most of all I should like to thank Mum and Dad, my family and Claire for their love and support.

To see more of Robert Davies's work go to www.robertdavies.uk.com. For more information about these images please email hospitalbob@hotmail.com